GOLD RUSH GONE WRONG

ARUN KUMAR

INDIA · SINGAPORE · MALAYSIA

ISBN
Paperback 979-8-89610-392-9
Hardcase 979-8-89632-830-8

Disclaimer

The contents of this book are based on the personal experiences and opinions of the author, Arun Kumar Verma. While every effort has been made to present accurate and truthful information, the events and incidents described are subject to the author's memory and interpretation. Names and identifying details may have been changed to protect the privacy of individuals involved.

This book is intended for informational and educational purposes only. It should not be considered professional legal, financial, or business advice. Readers are strongly encouraged to conduct their own research and consult with qualified professionals before making any decisions related to international business or gold trading.

The author and publisher disclaim any liability for any loss or damage incurred as a result of the information presented in this book. The reader assumes full responsibility for their actions, and the author does not guarantee the outcome of any similar endeavors.

Contents

Contents

Introduction:
A Golden Opportunity......?

My name is Arun Kumar Verma, and my story begins in the small town of Sitapur, in Uttar Pradesh, India. Growing up, life was simple, but I always had dreams bigger than my hometown. After completing my education locally, I found myself wanting more than just a job; I wanted a business that I could call my own. In 2017, while working at a footwear manufacturing company in Bahadurgarh, Haryana, I decided to start something on the side, something that could grow.

With a few resources, a bit of ambition, and a lot of late nights, I launched *Ambition Lifestyle,* an online business that sold garments, footwear, and lifestyle accessories. Leveraging platforms like Facebook and WhatsApp, I began reaching out to people, showcasing products, and, before long, I had a steady stream of customers. My online venture was thriving, and my confidence grew with every sale. *Ambition Lifestyle* was my first step into the world of business, and I was beginning to see the possibilities that lay beyond the boundaries of my job and my town.

It was during one of those routine days of managing orders and handling customer messages that I received a Facebook friend request from someone named Jhon. The profile picture showed a confident man, and his profile stated that he was originally from the Democratic Republic of Congo but living in Uganda. Out of curiosity, I accepted his request. Our initial conversations were casual, just greetings and exchanges about everyday life. He would tell me about Uganda, and I would share stories of India. Our chats were friendly, the kind that start small but gradually make you feel you're getting to know someone across borders.

After a few weeks, Jhon began to tell me about his business. He said he was involved in the trade of gold and painted a vivid picture of Uganda's rich gold reserves and the ease with which one could do business there. At first, I listened more out of interest than intent, as my own business was unrelated to the gold trade. But with each conversation, he seemed to peel back a layer of opportunity. According to Jhon, Uganda was a rising player in the gold trade, attracting investors from all over the world. He described a bustling market where small businesses could make significant profits, and he assured me that with his connections, I could enter this market smoothly.

Jhon's offer was tempting. He mentioned that he could get me the best prices and even offer credit terms, a unique opportunity designed, he said, to help new investors like myself. He suggested that I come to Uganda, visit his office, see the gold refinery firsthand, and witness the trade in action. The more he talked, the more I began to believe in this vision he was presenting. The potential profits in gold were far beyond what I was making in my current business, and the idea of expanding internationally was exhilarating.

During this time, I started connecting with others who were also interested in gold trading. Through Jhon's network, I was introduced to Govind, a businessman from Nepal, and Ram Kishan Lal, a jeweler from Kolkata, India. Both were experienced in gold jewelry manufacturing, and they, too, were captivated by the potential in Uganda. Together, we discussed the possibilities, analyzed the logistics, and shared our excitement. We saw this as more than just a business venture; it was a chance to establish something substantial, a rare opportunity that doesn't come along every day.

The idea of partnering with Jhon and his associates felt secure. He had experience, the right connections, and seemed genuinely invested in helping us succeed. His confidence and knowledge reassured me, and the more we spoke, the more I felt that he was someone I could trust. The prospect of witnessing gold refining, seeing the operations, and stepping into a world I'd only ever read about had me on the edge of my seat.

I spent weeks preparing for this trip. I bought gifts for Jhon and his team—clothes, watches, and other tokens of appreciation. This was my first international business trip, and I wanted to make a good impression. I had carefully planned everything: the arrangements, the meetings, and the logistics of sourcing gold from Uganda to sell in international markets. Every detail seemed to fall into place, and I was more convinced than ever that this was the right move.

Finally, on December 14, 2017, I boarded a flight from New Delhi to Entebbe International Airport in Uganda. The anticipation built up as I sat on that plane, thousands of feet above the ground, imagining the possibilities. This was it—the beginning of a journey that would transform my life. As we descended into Uganda, I looked out the window and felt a strange mix of excitement and unease, though I couldn't pinpoint why. Little did I know that this feeling would become a defining part of my journey.

Jhon met me at the airport with one of his colleagues. The warmth and enthusiasm they showed erased any lingering doubts I had.

They treated me like family, calling me their "younger brother" and ensuring I felt welcomed. We drove through Kampala, the capital of Uganda, and arrived at the Sheraton Kampala Hotel, where I would be staying. That evening, they took me out to dinner, and we discussed business plans over a hearty meal. They spoke about the vast potential of the gold trade, the profitability, and the opportunities for growth. By the end of the night, I was even more eager to dive into this new world.

The next morning, I visited Jhon's office. He introduced me to Mr. Patrick, the director of *Gold Soko Africa Ltd.* Mr. Patrick was a charismatic man, exuding the confidence and charm of a seasoned businessman. He explained the process of sourcing gold, how they refined it, and the legalities involved in exporting it. According to him, everything was by the book. They offered competitive pricing, flexible payment options, and even facilitated testing in government labs to assure quality. They promised me that as a buyer, I would be treated with the utmost transparency.

Mr. Patrick shared a structured plan for how they could handle the entire supply chain—from sourcing gold from mines to exporting it to my chosen destination. He mentioned that if needed, they could even send a representative with me to ensure the final testing and payment went smoothly. With all the procedures and assurances they laid out, it was hard not to feel a growing confidence in this venture.

Jhon and Mr. Patrick's approach seemed so genuine, so professional. They seemed to want me to succeed as much as I did. The security measures were tight; the office had guards armed with AK-47s, surveillance cameras, and high-level precautions in place. They showed me their storage facilities, filled with boxes of gold nuggets, and the government-certified documentation for every shipment. At that moment, surrounded by armed guards and the glitter of gold, I felt secure, reassured by the professionalism of it all.

Looking back, that trip to Uganda should have been a warning. But the charm, the confidence, and the seemingly legitimate setup clouded my judgment. I thought I was entering a world of immense opportunity, that my hard work was about to pay off in ways I had never imagined.

What followed, however, was a journey into deception and despair. It was a series of manipulations so intricate, I could hardly believe it was happening, even as it unraveled before me. The people I trusted, the plans I made, and the dreams I chased were about to crumble, revealing the harsh reality beneath the golden surface. This book is my story—a story of ambition, betrayal, and survival in a world that wasn't what it seemed. It's a story I'm sharing to help others see the hidden dangers behind the allure of easy fortune.

Chapter 1

The Connection on Facebook

It all began with a simple notification on my phone—a friend request from someone named Jhon. The profile picture showed a man with a confident smile, his background hinting at a life in Africa. Curious, I accepted the request, not knowing that this small click would change the entire course of my life. At that time, I was running my reselling business, *Ambition Lifestyle*, where I sold garments, footwear, and accessories online. Business was doing well, and I was comfortable with the life I was building. I had no idea that soon, everything was about to change.

Jhon and I started chatting casually. It began with harmless small talk—just greetings and simple exchanges about our lives. Jhon told me that he was from the Democratic Republic of Congo but currently living in Uganda. He said he worked in gold trading. At first, I thought it was just another online acquaintance, the kind you exchange pleasantries with occasionally but never think much about. However, Jhon had a way of keeping the conversation going, and soon, we were talking almost every day.

Over the next few weeks, our conversations evolved. Jhon spoke about his life in Uganda, the opportunities there, and the wealth that could be made if one knew where to look. He mentioned his involvement in the gold business, describing Uganda as a rich land filled with opportunities for those who dared to take a step into the unknown. The way he talked about gold—its value, its allure, and the money to be made—began to intrigue me. I listened, partly out of curiosity and partly because Jhon seemed so confident and genuine.

He spoke of gold mines, bustling markets, and the prospect of incredible profits. Uganda, he said, was a land full of potential, where those with ambition could thrive. Jhon's stories were captivating. He described a life that seemed so different from mine—a life filled with adventure, wealth, and endless opportunities. He told me how he worked directly with miners and how easy it was to buy gold at a good price, refine it, and sell it for a significant profit. There were many buyers, he assured me, and the business was booming.

Jhon often described his work in vivid detail. He would talk about his visits to the mines, the hardworking miners extracting gold from the earth, and the feeling of holding raw gold in his hands. He painted a picture of a thriving community where everyone worked together to bring gold from the depths of the ground to the global market. He spoke of the challenges involved, but he made it sound like the kind of challenge that was worth every effort. He emphasized how he had built strong relationships with the miners, how trust was at the core of the business, and how this trust was the foundation for success.

Over time, I found myself considering the possibility of getting involved. My reselling business was doing well, but the thought of stepping into something as lucrative as gold trading was tempting. Jhon made it sound easy. He assured me that he could guide me, that he had connections, and that he would help me every step of the way. The more we talked, the more I began to see myself stepping into this world. The idea of importing gold and making substantial profits began to take hold of me. It felt like a natural progression, a chance to take my business to the next level.

Jhon's offer seemed like a once-in-a-lifetime opportunity. He spoke of the potential to make profits beyond anything I had imagined, and he painted a picture of a business that was both exciting and rewarding. He even offered credit facilities to help me get started, assuring me that I wouldn't need to invest heavily upfront. It seemed like everything was falling into place, as if fate had brought Jhon into my life at just the right time.

By this point, Jhon and I had been talking for months, and I felt like I knew him well. He was friendly, supportive, and always willing to answer my questions. He had become more than just an online acquaintance; he was a mentor of sorts, someone who was guiding me toward something bigger. The more we talked, the more I trusted him. He spoke with confidence, and he seemed to know what he was doing. His experience in the gold business, his connections, and his willingness to help me made me feel like this was the right move.

Eventually, Jhon suggested that I visit Uganda to see everything for myself. He wanted me to meet his partners, see the gold, and witness how the business operated. He promised to show me the refineries, the mines, and introduce me to the people he worked with. The idea of traveling to Uganda was both thrilling and terrifying. It was a big step, but Jhon assured me that he would take care of everything—from the moment I landed to the moment I left. He made it sound like an adventure, an opportunity to see a new part of the world and step into a business that could change my life.

Jhon's excitement was contagious. He described the beautiful landscapes of Uganda, the bustling markets, and the vibrant culture. He spoke of the welcoming nature of the people and how they embraced those who came to do business. He even talked about the Ugandan food, the local delicacies that he couldn't wait for me to try. He made Uganda sound like a land of opportunity, a place where dreams could come true if one was willing to take a chance. I found myself getting excited about the trip—not just for the business opportunity, but for the experience of visiting a new country and immersing myself in a different culture.

Jhon also introduced me to some of his partners through online calls. They seemed professional, knowledgeable, and just as eager to get started as I was. They spoke about the processes involved in the gold trade—the sourcing, refining, and exporting. They emphasized the safety measures, the legal protocols, and the steps they took to ensure that everything was above board. It all seemed so well-organized, and their professionalism further convinced me that this was a legitimate opportunity. They talked about the success they had seen with previous clients, and they assured me that I could expect the same.

As the weeks turned into months, I found myself spending more and more time talking to Jhon and his partners. They had become a part of my daily routine, and the idea of getting into the gold business had taken root in my mind. I began to make plans—thinking about the logistics, the potential profits, and the ways in which this new venture could transform my life. I started to envision a future where I was not just reselling products online, but dealing in gold, making deals across borders, and expanding my business beyond anything I had ever imagined.

And so, after months of talking, planning, and dreaming, I made the decision. I was going to Uganda. I was going to see this world that Jhon had described so vividly, and I was going to take a step into the unknown. Little did I know that this journey, which began with a simple friend request on Facebook, would lead me down a path filled with deception, betrayal, and loss. This was the beginning of my journey—a journey that would test me in ways I never imagined.

The preparations for the trip were filled with excitement. I remember packing my bags, buying gifts for Jhon and his partners—small tokens of appreciation for the people who were about to help me embark on this incredible journey. I booked my flight, made arrangements for my stay, and mentally prepared myself for what was to come. I told my friends and family that I was going on a business trip, though I didn't go into too much detail. I wanted to keep things under wraps until I was sure of what lay ahead. But deep inside, I felt a mix of excitement and nervousness. This was the biggest step I had ever taken in my life, and I was ready to see where it would lead.

The day finally came when I boarded the plane to Uganda. As the plane took off, I looked out the window and felt a rush of emotions—excitement, hope, and a hint of fear. I was leaving behind the familiar, stepping into a new world with new possibilities. I didn't know what awaited me in Uganda, but I was ready to find out. I was ready to take the risk, to chase the dream that Jhon had painted for me. Little did I know that this dream would soon turn into a nightmare, and that the journey I was embarking on would be one of the most challenging experiences of my life.

Looking back, I realize how naive I was. I wanted so badly to believe in the opportunity, to trust in the people who seemed so genuine. I didn't see the warning signs, the small inconsistencies that should have made me question everything. But at that moment, all I saw was the promise of something bigger, something better. And so, I took the leap, unaware of the darkness that lay ahead. This was just the beginning—a beginning that would lead me down a path filled with hard lessons, painful losses, and ultimately, a story that needed to be told.

Chapter 2

The Proposal of a Lifetime

My excitement about visiting Uganda and entering the gold trade had reached a fever pitch. Jhon had painted such a vivid picture of what awaited me there—the opportunities, the connections, and the wealth that could be gained. For weeks, all I could think about was what lay ahead. When I finally landed in Entebbe, Uganda, it felt like stepping into a new world, full of promise and potential. The airport was bustling, a mix of locals and travelers, and I could feel the energy in the air. Everything felt like an adventure, and I was ready to dive in.

Jhon was waiting for me at the airport, just as he had promised. He greeted me with a warm smile and a firm handshake, and immediately, I felt at ease. He introduced me to his colleague, who was there to assist with my visit, and they both treated me like an old friend. We drove through the streets of Kampala, Uganda's capital city, and I couldn't help but be fascinated by the sights and sounds around me. The city was alive, full of activity and color, and it felt like a place where anything was possible. Jhon pointed out various landmarks as we drove, talking enthusiastically about the country, the people, and, of course, the gold trade.

We arrived at my hotel, the Sheraton Kampala, which was a beautiful, upscale place that made me feel even more confident about the journey ahead. After settling in, we had our first in-person business discussion over dinner. Jhon spoke passionately about the opportunities that awaited me and introduced me to his colleague, Mr. Patrick, the director of Gold Soko Africa Ltd. Mr. Patrick was charismatic and spoke with an air of authority. He explained how the gold trade worked—the sourcing, the refining, and the exporting—and how everything was done in a legal and structured manner. He emphasized their transparency, the importance of trust, and how they valued long-term relationships with their clients.

Listening to Mr. Patrick and Jhon, I felt reassured. They spoke with such confidence, such ease, that it was hard not to believe every word they said. Mr. Patrick talked about the gold mines, the process of extracting and refining the gold, and the opportunities for profit that were waiting for someone with the courage to take a chance. He explained the structure of their business, their partnership with miners in DRC Congo, and their connections with buyers in other markets. Everything seemed to be in place—a well-oiled machine that was already operating successfully, just waiting for someone like me to come on board.

The next morning, Jhon and Mr. Patrick took me to visit their office. It was a modest but professional setup, with security guards at the entrance and people busy with paperwork and other activities inside. They introduced me to their team, a group of people who were polite, professional, and welcoming. They showed me the documents they used for export, certificates of authenticity, and the testing reports for the gold. I was impressed by the level of organization and the apparent legitimacy of their operation. It felt like I was stepping into a world that was both exciting and secure.

One of the most convincing aspects of the entire setup was the promise of gold testing in government-certified labs. Mr. Patrick assured me that every batch of gold was tested to confirm its purity, and buyers were welcome to witness the process. He even offered to take me to one of these labs to see the testing firsthand. This transparency was exactly what I needed to feel comfortable moving forward. It was clear that they were doing everything by the book, and that gave me the confidence I needed to take the next step.

After the office visit, Jhon and Mr. Patrick invited me to lunch at a popular local restaurant. Over plates of delicious Ugandan food, they continued to share their experiences and stories of the gold business. They spoke about the challenges they had faced and overcome, and how those challenges had made them stronger and more determined. They painted a picture of a business that was built on hard work, trust, and mutual benefit. They made me feel like I was already part of their team, and that together, we could achieve great things.

It wasn't long before we started discussing the specifics of our partnership. Jhon and Mr. Patrick discussed the potential of exporting gold, and I began to think of how I could enter this business in a way that aligned with legal requirements. Instead of directly investing in a shipment with them, I realized that I needed to fully understand the processes involved, especially if I wanted to bring gold into India legally. I knew that I had to explore all the legal avenues for importing gold from Africa to India, ensuring that everything was done according to the regulations.

The plan seemed straightforward: I would work with Jhon and Mr. Patrick to understand the logistics of exporting gold, and we would prepare a shipment plan that could eventually lead to legal imports into India. They assured me that they had done this many times before, and everything appeared to be in place. However, instead of committing financially at that stage, I decided to focus on planning and understanding the legal framework needed for future shipments. They spoke with such confidence and experience that I had no reason to doubt them.

To further reassure me, Jhon and Mr. Patrick took me to visit a gold storage facility. It was a secure location, guarded by armed personnel, and I had to register my name and pay a small fee to gain entry. Inside, they showed me several boxes filled with gold nuggets, each carefully labeled and documented. They allowed me to take a sample of the gold, which we then took to a government-certified lab for testing. The results came back as 96% pure, 22-carat gold—exactly as they had promised. This level of transparency and the apparent legitimacy of the entire process made me feel like I was making the right decision.

As the days went by, I found myself becoming more and more involved in the planning process. Jhon and Mr. Patrick included me in their meetings, introduced me to their contacts, and made me feel like a valued partner.

They explained every detail of the export process—the documentation, the customs procedures, and the logistics of transporting the gold. They assured me that they had everything under control and that all I needed to do was trust them and follow their lead.

The excitement of being part of something so big was exhilarating. I had always dreamed of expanding my business, of doing something that would take me to the next level, and this felt like the perfect opportunity. Jhon and Mr. Patrick made me feel like I was part of a family, a team that was working together toward a common goal. They spoke about the future, about the potential for growth, and about the wealth that awaited us if we were successful. It was hard not to get caught up in their enthusiasm, and I found myself fully committed to the plan.

One evening, after a long day of meetings and planning, Jhon and Mr. Patrick invited me to a local bar to relax and unwind. It was a lively place, filled with music, laughter, and people enjoying themselves. As we sat there, sipping our drinks and talking about the future, I couldn't help but feel a sense of excitement and anticipation. I was on the verge of something incredible, something that could change my life forever. The camaraderie, the sense of adventure, and the promise of success made me feel like I was exactly where I was meant to be.

We spent the next few days going over the logistics and planning in detail. My primary goal was to understand how I could legally import gold into India, what licenses I would need, and what regulations I needed to comply with. Jhon and Mr. Patrick were enthusiastic and eager to help, assuring me that they would guide me through every step. It all seemed so promising, and I was eager to move forward with a solid plan in place.

As the planning continued, I felt a mix of emotions. There was excitement, of course, but there was also a sense of nervousness. This was a big step, and I was putting a lot of trust in people I had only known for a few months. But every time I felt a hint of doubt, Jhon and Mr. Patrick were there to reassure me. They spoke with such confidence, such certainty, that it was impossible not to believe them. They had shown me the gold, introduced me to their contacts, and included me in every step of the process. I had no reason to doubt them, and so I pushed any lingering fears aside.

This was it—the beginning of a new chapter, a new opportunity, and a new life. At that moment, all I knew was that I was taking a step into the unknown, chasing a dream that I believed was within my reach.

Chapter 3

The Partnerships Formed

With my confidence growing, the next step was to figure out exactly how I could make this venture a reality. My conversations with Jhon and Mr. Patrick had already set the foundation, and now it was time to bring others on board who could help turn this vision into something concrete. I knew that in order to make the most of the opportunity in Uganda, I needed partners—people who had experience, resources, and the same drive for success that I had. That's when I reached out to two individuals who I thought could be the perfect fit.

The first person I contacted was Govind, a businessman from Nepal. Govind and I had connected online through mutual business interests. He had a background in dealing with precious metals and was well-versed in the complexities of the international market. I had always been impressed by his knowledge and his approach to business, and I felt that he would be interested in the opportunity to expand his operations beyond Nepal. When I told Govind about the possibilities in Uganda, he was immediately intrigued. The idea of sourcing gold directly from Africa at competitive prices and selling it in the international market was something that resonated with him, and he was eager to hear more.

Govind and I spent several hours discussing the potential of the gold trade in Uganda. He asked detailed questions about my meetings with Jhon and Mr. Patrick, and I shared everything I had learned so far—the process of extracting and refining the gold, the logistics of exporting it, and the testing that was done to ensure quality. Govind was thorough in his approach, and I could see that he was already calculating the risks and rewards in his mind. By the end of our conversation, Govind agreed to come on board. He believed that with his experience and my connection to Jhon and Mr. Patrick, we could make this venture a success.

The next person I reached out to was Ram Kishan Lal, an experienced jeweler from Kolkata, India. Ram Kishan was an expert in gold and had been running a successful jewelry business for decades. He had a deep understanding of the gold market in India, and I knew that his knowledge and expertise would be invaluable. I called Ram Kishan and explained the opportunity that I had stumbled upon. He listened carefully as I described my meetings in Uganda, the connections I had made, and the potential profits that could be gained by sourcing gold directly from Africa.

Ram Kishan was intrigued but cautious. He had seen many opportunities come and go, and he knew that the gold business was fraught with challenges. He asked me about the legalities of importing gold into India, the certifications that were required, and the reliability of my contacts in Uganda. I appreciated his cautious approach because it forced me to think critically about every aspect of the venture. I reassured him that everything I had seen so far appeared to be legitimate, and I told him about the government-certified testing, the documentation, and the professionalism of Jhon and Mr. Patrick. After several discussions, Ram Kishan agreed to join the venture, but he made it clear that he wanted to be involved in every step of the process to ensure that everything was done by the book.

With Govind and Ram Kishan on board, we began to lay the groundwork for our partnership. We decided that each of us would bring our unique strengths to the table—Govind's experience in international trade, Ram Kishan's expertise in the gold market, and my connection to Jhon and Mr. Patrick in Uganda. Together, we believed that we had the right combination of skills, knowledge, and resources to make this venture a success.

The first step in our partnership was to establish clear roles and responsibilities. Govind would be responsible for handling the logistics of transporting the gold from Uganda to its destination. He had experience dealing with customs, shipping companies, and the various challenges that came with moving valuable goods across borders. His role would be crucial in ensuring that the gold was transported safely and efficiently. Ram Kishan, on the other hand, would be responsible for evaluating the quality of the gold and handling the sale of the gold once it reached Dubai. His expertise in gold refining and his connections in the jewelry market would ensure that we got the best possible price for our product.

My role was to stay in Uganda, work closely with Jhon and Mr. Patrick, and oversee the sourcing and refining of the gold. I would be the point of contact on the ground, ensuring that everything went according to plan and that we were getting the best possible quality. It was a big responsibility, but I was ready for the challenge. I had already seen the operation firsthand, and I trusted Jhon and Mr. Patrick to deliver on their promises.

We held regular meetings—sometimes in person, sometimes over video calls—to discuss our progress and plan our next steps. The more we talked, the more confident we became that we were on the right track. We reviewed the legal requirements for importing gold into India, the licenses we needed, and the procedures we had to follow. However, we soon realized that the process was far more complicated and costly than we had anticipated. The cost of obtaining the necessary licenses and complying with all the regulations was becoming prohibitively high, and it was clear that importing gold into India would be a challenging endeavor. Given these increasing costs and regulatory challenges, we decided to explore an alternative: exporting the gold to Dubai instead. Dubai had a well-established market for gold, with fewer regulatory hurdles, making it a more practical option for our initial venture. We were determined to avoid any shortcuts that could jeopardize our business, and this change in strategy seemed like the best way forward.

One of the biggest challenges we faced was navigating the regulatory landscape for importing gold into India. The Indian government had strict regulations in place, and we needed to make sure that we complied with all of them. We learned that importing gold required specific licenses and that there were limits on the amount of gold that could be brought into the country. We also needed to work with banks and authorized agencies to facilitate the import process. It was a complex web of requirements, but we were committed to doing everything the right way.

Govind, Ram Kishan, and I spent countless hours researching the regulations, talking to experts, and reaching out to contacts who could help us navigate the process. We spoke to officials at the Metal and Mineral Trading Corporation (MMTC) in New Delhi, which was one of the authorized agencies for importing gold into India. They provided us with valuable information about the licenses we needed and the steps we had to take to ensure compliance. It was a lot of work, but we knew that it was necessary if we wanted to succeed.

As we continued our preparations, I spent more time with Jhon and Mr. Patrick, learning everything I could about their operation. They took me to visit the gold mines, where I saw firsthand the hard work that went into extracting the gold from the earth. The miners worked long hours in difficult conditions, using both traditional methods and modern equipment to extract the precious metal. It was a labor-intensive process, and it gave me a new appreciation for the value of the gold that we were dealing with.

Jhon also took me to visit the refinery where the gold was processed. The refinery was a modest facility, but it was equipped with everything needed to refine the gold to the highest standards. I watched as the raw gold was melted down, purified, and molded into bars. The entire process was fascinating, and it gave me a better understanding of the journey that the gold took from the mine to the market. Mr. Patrick was always there to answer my questions, and he explained each step of the refining process in detail.

The more I learned, the more confident I became in our ability to make this venture a success. Jhon and Mr. Patrick were knowledgeable, experienced, and seemed genuinely committed to helping us succeed. They introduced me to their network of contacts, including local officials, customs agents, and other players in the gold trade. It was clear that they had built strong relationships in the industry, and I felt reassured knowing that we had them on our side.

One of the most important aspects of our preparation was ensuring that we had a reliable buyer for the gold once it arrived in Dubai. Ram Kishan took the lead on this front, reaching out to his contacts in the Dubai gold market to gauge their interest. The response was overwhelmingly positive. Gold was always in high demand, and the prospect of sourcing it directly from Africa at competitive prices was appealing to many of Ram Kishan's contacts. He received several tentative offers, and we felt confident that we would have no trouble selling the gold once it arrived in India.

As we approached the final stages of our planning, we faced a few unexpected challenges. One of the biggest issues was securing the necessary financing to cover the costs of the operation. While we had all agreed to contribute our own funds, the scale of the venture required additional capital. We explored various options, including loans from banks and investments from private individuals. After much discussion, we decided to bring in a fourth partner—Rahul, a businessman based in Dubai who had experience in international trade and was willing to invest in our venture.

Rahul's involvement brought a new level of expertise and financial backing to our partnership. He had experience dealing with customs, shipping, and the complexities of international trade, and he was eager to be part of our venture. With Rahul on board, we felt that we had all the pieces in place. Each of us brought something unique to the table, and together, we believed that we could overcome any challenge that came our way.

The final step before moving forward was to conduct a trial run. We decided to start with a small shipment of gold to test the waters and ensure that everything went smoothly. The plan was for me to work closely with Jhon and Mr. Patrick to source the gold, while Govind handled the logistics of transportation, and Ram Kishan worked on securing buyers in Dubai. Rahul would oversee the financial aspects and ensure that we had the necessary funding to cover all expenses.

The trial run was critical; it would allow us to identify any potential issues and address them before committing to a larger shipment. We wanted to make sure that we had covered all our bases and that we were fully prepared for any challenges that might arise. We spent weeks finalizing the details, double-checking our paperwork, and coordinating with our contacts in Uganda, India, and Dubai.

Finally, the day arrived when we were ready to move forward with the trial run. I felt a mix of excitement and nervousness as I prepared for the shipment. This was the culmination of months of planning, discussions, and hard work, and I was eager to see it all come together. We had done everything we could to ensure that the operation was successful, and now it was time to put our plan to the test.

As I stood there, watching the gold being prepared for transport, I couldn't help but feel a sense of pride. This was a big step for me.

Chapter 4

Stepping Foot in Uganda

The day had finally arrived for my first visit to Uganda. After months of discussions with Jhon over Facebook, I was eager to meet him in person and see for myself the opportunities he had spoken so passionately about. My journey to Uganda was not just about exploring a new business venture; it was also about stepping into an entirely new world, filled with unknowns. I boarded my flight with a mix of excitement and nervousness, hopeful that what awaited me would be worth the leap of faith I was taking.

I arrived at Entebbe International Airport in the evening. The air was warm and humid, and the airport was bustling with people from all walks of life. As I made my way through the terminal, I spotted Jhon waiting for me with a broad smile on his face. He greeted me warmly, and I could immediately feel his enthusiasm and eagerness to make me feel at home. There was a sense of comfort in his presence, as if we were old friends finally meeting after a long time. He introduced me to his colleague, and they both assured me that they had everything arranged for my stay.

We made our way to Kampala, the capital city of Uganda. During the drive, Jhon pointed out different landmarks, spoke about the culture, and shared stories about life in Uganda. The city was lively, with bustling markets, busy streets, and a unique blend of modern and traditional influences. It was a vibrant place, full of energy, and I couldn't help but feel a sense of excitement. Everything seemed new and fascinating, and I was eager to learn more about the country that would play such a significant role in my life moving forward.

Jhon took me to my hotel, the Sheraton Kampala, where I would be staying during my time in Uganda. The hotel was beautiful, and the staff were friendly and welcoming.

After checking in, Jhon and his colleague invited me to join them for dinner at a local restaurant. As we sat down for the meal, I felt a sense of camaraderie. Jhon spoke passionately about the gold trade, about the opportunities it presented, and how he believed we could build something truly successful together. His excitement was contagious, and I found myself getting caught up in his vision of what was possible.

The next morning, Jhon arrived at my hotel to take me to meet Mr. Patrick, the director of Gold Soko Africa Ltd. This was the moment I had been waiting for—the chance to meet the people behind the operation, to see firsthand what they were doing, and to understand how it all worked. We drove to the office, and as we arrived, I was struck by how professional everything appeared. The building was modest but well-maintained, with security guards at the entrance and people moving purposefully inside.

Jhon introduced me to Mr. Patrick, a tall, confident man who exuded authority. He welcomed me warmly and spoke about the work they were doing. He explained the process of sourcing gold from the DRC Congo, refining it in Uganda, and exporting it to international markets. As he spoke, I could sense his pride in the operation they had built, and it was clear that he was serious about maintaining high standards. He emphasized their commitment to quality, transparency, and building long-term relationships with their partners.

Mr. Patrick gave me a tour of their facilities, showing me the refinery and the storage area where the gold was kept. The setup was impressive, and everything seemed to be in place. I could see workers busy at their tasks, refining the raw gold into a purer form, and documenting every step of the process. The security measures were stringent, with armed guards stationed at key points and strict access controls in place. It all looked legitimate and professional, and I began to feel a growing sense of confidence that this was a genuine opportunity.

Over the next few days, I continued to meet with Jhon, Mr. Patrick, and other members of the team at Gold Soko Africa Ltd. They took me to visit the gold storage facilities, where I was shown the gold that had been sourced from the DRC Congo. The storage area was heavily guarded, and every detail—weight, origin, and quality—was meticulously recorded. They even allowed me to take a small sample of the gold, which I would later have tested at a government-certified lab. This level of transparency was reassuring, and it helped to build my confidence in the legitimacy of the venture.

Jhon also took me to visit some of the local mining sites, where I had the chance to see firsthand the hard work that went into extracting the gold from the earth. The miners were hardworking individuals, dedicated to their craft, and it was clear that they took pride in what they were doing. Seeing the entire process—from extraction to refining to storage—gave me a better understanding of the value chain and the effort that went into producing the gold. It was an eye-opening experience, and it reinforced my belief that this was a business worth pursuing.

As my time in Uganda progressed, I found myself growing more comfortable with the people I was working with and the environment

I was in. The warmth of Jhon's welcome, the professionalism of Mr. Patrick and his team, and the seemingly legitimate setup of the entire operation made everything appear promising. There were, of course, still questions in my mind—uncertainties that came with stepping into a new industry in a foreign country—but the initial impressions were positive, and I was determined to see where this opportunity could take me.

One of the key moments during my visit was when Jhon and Mr. Patrick took me to meet with some local government officials. They emphasized the importance of maintaining good relationships with the authorities, as this was crucial for ensuring the smooth operation of the business. The officials we met with were polite and professional, and they seemed supportive of the work that Gold Soko Africa Ltd was doing. This further reinforced my belief that the venture was legitimate and that we were on the right track.

By the end of my visit, I had developed a sense of trust in Jhon, Mr. Patrick, and the entire operation. The initial positive impressions had grown into a genuine belief that this was a real opportunity, one that could be both profitable and impactful. The professionalism, transparency, and commitment to quality that I had seen during my time in Uganda gave me the confidence to take the next steps. I was ready to move forward, to invest my time, energy, and resources into building a successful gold trading business.

Stepping foot in Uganda had been a leap of faith, but it was a leap that had paid off. I had found partners I could trust, a business that seemed promising, and an opportunity that I was eager to pursue. As I prepared to return home, I felt a renewed sense of purpose. The journey ahead would not be easy, and there were sure to be challenges along the way, but I was ready to face them head-on. This was just the beginning, and I was determined to make the most of it.

Chapter 5

Meeting the Experts at Gold Soko Africa Ltd

The trial run was moving forward, with a shipment of 25 kilograms of gold at a price of $24,000 per kilogram. The market price at the time ranged between $29,000 and $30,000 per kilogram, presenting us with a promising profit margin. The anticipation was almost tangible. I was eager to learn and absorb every bit of knowledge I could about the gold trade, and Jhon and Mr. Patrick were keen on showing me the depth of the business. As part of our preparations, they arranged for me to meet some of the key people involved in the day-to-day operations at Gold Soko Africa Ltd. These experts would help me understand every facet of the process—from sourcing to refining to preparing for export.

The first meeting was with Mr. Musanganya S. Patrick, the director of Gold Soko Africa Ltd. Though I had already met him briefly, this time it was a more detailed, in-depth conversation about the gold mining and refining business. Mr. Patrick was an impressive man—tall, with a deep voice that commanded attention. He had the kind of presence that made you feel like you were in the company of someone who truly knew his industry inside and out.

We sat in his office, a modest yet well-furnished space with various maps of Uganda and the surrounding regions pinned to the walls. Each map was marked with highlighted areas, which I later learned were locations of various gold mining sites and partner operations. As we sat down, Mr. Patrick opened a large binder filled with documents, licenses, and certifications. He began to explain the legal requirements for operating a gold refining and export business in Uganda. He spoke about the importance of government certifications, the need for proper permits, and how they ensured every step of their operation adhered to the country's legal framework.

"In this business, transparency is everything," he said, looking directly at me. "We work with several government bodies to ensure that every gram of gold that leaves our refinery is legitimate and that all taxes and duties are paid. Trust is our most important asset."

It was clear that Mr. Patrick was very thorough, and he emphasized the importance of doing things the right way. He explained that Gold Soko Africa Ltd worked closely with miners from the DRC Congo, many of whom brought raw gold into Uganda for refining and export. The partnerships they had established with these miners were built on mutual trust, and Gold Soko Africa Ltd provided them with fair compensation for their work. He showed me the contracts they had with different mining operations, which outlined the terms of their partnership and the standards they adhered to.

After my conversation with Mr. Patrick, he introduced me to the head of refining, Mr. Okello. Mr. Okello was a soft-spoken man in his late forties, with a wealth of experience in metallurgy. He had been working in the gold refining industry for over two decades and had an intimate understanding of the entire process. Mr. Okello took me on a tour of the refinery, explaining each stage of the refining process in detail.

The refining process was meticulous. Mr. Okello explained that the raw gold was first weighed and documented before being melted down in large furnaces. The gold was then mixed with specific chemicals to remove impurities, leaving behind 96% pure, 22-carat gold. I watched as workers, clad in protective gear, carefully poured the molten gold into molds, forming small bars.

"Every batch is tested multiple times," Mr. Okello said, pointing to a section of the refinery where technicians were conducting purity tests. "We use both fire assay and X-ray fluorescence testing to ensure the quality of our gold. It's crucial that we maintain a consistent level of purity, as our reputation depends on it."

As I observed the workers and listened to Mr. Okello's explanations, I couldn't help but be impressed by the level of precision and care that went into each step. The workers moved with practiced ease, their focus unwavering as they handled the valuable metal. It was clear that this was not just a job for them—it was a craft, one that required skill, patience, and a deep understanding of the material they were working with.

Mr. Okello also spoke about the importance of safety in the refinery. He explained the protocols they had in place to protect the workers from the hazards associated with the refining process. The fumes produced during the melting and chemical treatment stages were carefully vented through a sophisticated exhaust system, and the workers were provided with high-quality protective equipment to ensure their safety.

After touring the refinery, I was introduced to Ms. Achieng, the head of logistics and export. Ms. Achieng was a sharp, efficient woman who was responsible for coordinating the transportation of the refined gold from the refinery to the airport, and ultimately to its final destination. She walked me through the documentation process, showing me the various forms and permits required for each shipment. There were export licenses, certificates of origin, packing lists, and airway bills—each document meticulously prepared and verified to ensure compliance with both Ugandan law and international trade regulations.

Ms. Achieng also explained the importance of working closely with customs officials to avoid any delays or complications during the export process. She had built strong relationships with key personnel at the Entebbe International Airport, which helped ensure that their shipments moved smoothly through customs. "In this business, timing is everything," she said. "A delay at customs can cost us not only money but also our reputation. We make sure everything is in order before the gold even leaves the refinery."

The level of detail involved in the logistics of exporting gold was staggering. Ms. Achieng's role was crucial, as even the smallest mistake in the paperwork could lead to significant delays or even the seizure of a shipment. She showed me how they tracked each shipment, from the moment it left the refinery to the moment it arrived at its destination. Every step was documented, and every precaution was taken to ensure that the gold reached its buyer safely and on time.

One of the most eye-opening aspects of my time at Gold Soko Africa Ltd was the realization of just how interconnected every part of the operation was. From the miners in the DRC Congo to the refinery workers, the logistics team, and the customs officials—everyone played a vital role in ensuring the success of the business. It was a complex web of relationships, each one built on trust, expertise, and a shared goal of bringing gold to the international market.

Over the next few days, I continued to spend time at the refinery, learning as much as I could from the experts there. I watched as they conducted assays, analyzed samples, and prepared shipments for export. I asked countless questions, and each one was met with a patient and detailed response. It was clear that the people at Gold Soko Africa Ltd took great pride in their work, and they were more than willing to share their knowledge with me.

During one of our discussions, Mr. Patrick spoke to me about the challenges they faced in the gold trade. He explained that while the potential for profit was significant, the risks were equally high. The gold industry was fraught with challenges—from fluctuating market prices to the constant threat of fraud and theft. "You have to be vigilant at all times," he said. "One mistake can cost you everything. That's why we take every precaution, and why we work only with people we trust."

Mr. Patrick's words stayed with me. It was a reminder that while the gold trade offered immense opportunities, it was not without its dangers. Trust was a recurring theme in every conversation I had at Gold Soko Africa Ltd—trust between the miners and the refinery, trust between the refinery and the buyers, and trust between the partners involved in the business. Without trust, the entire operation would fall apart.

I also had the opportunity to meet with some of the miners who supplied gold to Gold Soko Africa Ltd. These were hardworking men, many of whom had spent their entire lives working in the mines. They spoke about the difficulties they faced—long hours, dangerous working conditions, and the constant uncertainty of whether they would strike a rich vein or come up empty-handed. Despite the challenges, there was a sense of pride in what they did. They knew that their work was an essential part of a much larger operation, and they took pride in the fact that they were helping to bring gold to the world.

One miner, a man named Jean-Pierre, told me about his experiences working in the DRC Congo. He described the arduous journey from the mining sites to the refinery, often through difficult terrain and in challenging conditions. "It's not easy work," he said, "but it's what we do. We know the risks, and we know the rewards. We do this to provide for our families, to give them a better life."

Hearing Jean-Pierre's story gave me a new perspective on the gold trade. It was easy to get caught up in the excitement of the potential profits and the allure of the gold itself, but it was important to remember the people who made it all possible. The miners, the refinery workers, the logistics team—they were the backbone of the entire operation, and without them, none of it would be possible.

As my time at Gold Soko Africa Ltd continued, I began to feel more and more like a part of the team. I had come to Uganda with the goal of understanding the gold trade, and I felt that I was finally beginning to grasp the intricacies of the business. Jhon and Mr. Patrick had been true to their word - they had given me access to every part of their operation, and they had been open and transparent about the challenges and risks involved.

By the end of my stay, I had developed a deep respect for the people at Gold Soko Africa Ltd and the work they did. They were professionals in every sense of the word, and they were committed to doing things the right way. It was clear that they had built a reputation for integrity and reliability, and they were determined to maintain that reputation at all costs.

As I prepared to leave the refinery and return to my hotel, Mr. Patrick pulled me aside. "Arun," he said, "I know this business can seem overwhelming at times. There are a lot of moving parts, and there are a lot of risks. But if you stay focused, if you surround yourself with the right people, and if you always do things the right way, you can succeed. We're glad to have you as part of our team, and we're looking forward to working with you."

His words meant a lot to me. I knew that I still had a long way to go, and there was still much to learn, but I felt ready to take the next step. The journey ahead would not be easy, but I was determined to see it through. I had the support of my partners, the expertise of the team at Gold Soko Africa Ltd, and a growing understanding of the gold trade. I was ready to move forward, one step at a time, toward the goal we had set for ourselves.

As I left the refinery that day, I felt a renewed sense of purpose. The road ahead was uncertain, and there were sure to be challenges along the way, but I was confident that we had the right team and the right plan in place. The gold trade was a complex and demanding business, but with the knowledge and experience I had gained, I felt ready to take on whatever lay ahead. The next chapter of my journey was about to begin, and I was ready to face it head-on.

Chapter 6

The Test of Trust

After spending significant time with Jhon and Mr. Patrick in Uganda, it was finally time to put my newfound knowledge to the test. The next crucial step was to evaluate the quality of the gold through an official government lab. This would be the defining moment that would determine whether the venture was truly as promising as it seemed or if there were hidden pitfalls yet to be discovered.

The morning we planned to conduct the sample testing was a mixture of anticipation and anxiety. Jhon, Mr. Patrick, and I gathered at the refinery, ready to take the sample of gold to the government lab for analysis. This wasn't just about confirming the quality of the product; it was also about establishing trust with each other and verifying the legitimacy of the business. In the gold trade, trust is the cornerstone of every deal, and this lab test was the first major step in building that trust.

The sample we selected consisted of several nuggets that had been carefully documented and cataloged by the team at Gold Soko Africa Ltd. Every detail—weight, purity, origin—had been meticulously recorded to ensure that there would be no discrepancies later on. Once the sample was ready, we made our way to the government lab in Kampala. The journey to the lab felt longer than it actually was. My mind was filled with questions and doubts. What if the quality wasn't as high as Mr. Patrick had claimed? What if there were discrepancies that we couldn't resolve? These thoughts were hard to ignore, but I knew that I had to stay focused.

Upon arriving at the lab, we were greeted by a team of technicians who specialized in testing precious metals. The lab itself was a sterile environment, filled with specialized equipment designed to measure the purity of gold with incredible accuracy. The technicians took the sample and began their analysis, using both fire assay and X-ray fluorescence testing to determine its composition. I watched closely as they worked, each step feeling like an eternity. The entire process took several hours, and the atmosphere in the lab was tense as we waited for the results.

Finally, the technicians called us over to review their findings. The report showed that the gold was 96% pure, 22-carat, just as Mr. Patrick had promised. Seeing those results was an incredible relief. All the doubts that had been swirling in my mind began to fade away, replaced by a growing sense of confidence. The test results confirmed that the gold was of high-quality and that we were dealing with a genuine opportunity. It was the validation I needed to move forward with the venture.

Mr. Patrick was visibly pleased with the results, and he spoke about the importance of maintaining these standards for future shipments. "This is just the beginning," he said. "If we continue to deliver quality like this, we'll build a reputation that will open doors for us in the international market." His words resonated with me. This was indeed just the beginning, and I was determined to do everything in my power to ensure that our venture lived up to its potential.

With the test results in hand, we returned to the refinery. The mood was markedly different now—there was a sense of optimism and excitement that hadn't been there before. The successful testing had reinforced my belief that this was a legitimate and profitable opportunity, and I felt a renewed sense of purpose. I was ready to move forward, to take the next steps in building a successful gold trading business.

The next few days were spent finalizing the details of our partnership. I continued to work closely with Mr. Patrick and Jhon, learning more about the processes involved in refining, documenting, and preparing the gold for export. The trust we were building was crucial—not only between us but also with our future buyers and partners. The successful test had laid the foundation, but there was still much work to be done.

One of the key aspects of our preparations was ensuring that the refining process maintained the high standards that had been confirmed by the lab test. I spent hours at the refinery, observing the workers as they refined the raw gold into bars, ensuring that each step was carried out with precision and care. Mr. Okello, the head of refining, was meticulous in his approach, and his dedication to quality gave me confidence that we could consistently produce gold of the highest standard.

In addition to overseeing the refining process, I also began working with Ms. Achieng, who was responsible for coordinating the logistics of our future shipments. We discussed the documentation required for exporting the gold, including export licenses, certificates of origin, and packing lists. Ms. Achieng was incredibly knowledgeable, and her expertise was invaluable in helping me understand the complexities of international trade. I knew that the success of our venture depended not only on the quality of the gold but also on our ability to navigate the regulatory landscape and ensure that everything was done by the book.

The successful testing of the gold had also strengthened my relationships with Govind and Ram Kishan. They had been waiting anxiously for the results, and when I shared the news with them, they were both relieved and excited. The confirmation of the gold's quality was the assurance they needed to move forward with their roles in the venture. Govind, who would be handling logistics in Dubai, and Ram Kishan, who would be responsible for securing buyers, were both eager to take the next steps.

The trust that had been established through the successful testing was the foundation upon which we built our partnership. It was a reminder that in the gold trade, every detail matters, and there is no room for shortcuts. The testing had proven that we were dealing with a genuine opportunity, but it had also shown me the importance of due diligence and the need to verify every aspect of the business.

As we moved forward, I knew that there would be more challenges to face. The gold trade was complex, and there were many factors beyond our control that could impact our success.

However, the successful testing had given me the confidence to face those challenges head-on. I was ready to take the next steps, to continue building the business, and to turn the opportunity into a reality. This was the test of trust, and we had passed it. Now, it was time to move forward and take our venture to new heights.

Planning the First Shipment

After my extensive time spent with the experts at Gold Soko Africa Ltd, I felt a new surge of confidence. My understanding of the gold trade had grown significantly, and I was eager to put all that knowledge into practice. The plan was in motion, and we were finally ready to start preparing for our first official shipment. This was the moment that Govind, Ram Kishan, and I had been waiting for, and we were determined to get every detail right. We knew that our first shipment was crucial—it would set the tone for the future of our venture and prove our ability to execute in this complex industry.

The first shipment we planned was for 25 kilograms of 96% pure, 22-carat gold, with an initial cost of $24,000 per kilogram. We paid a 7% advance, amounting to $42,000, to cover initial documentation and export fees per kilogram. Given the current market price, which ranged from $29,000 to $30,000 per kilogram, the profit margins were promising. But beyond the numbers, it was essential for us to make sure the entire process—from refining to transport to export—went smoothly and complied with all the legal and regulatory requirements. We couldn't afford any mistakes, especially not with a shipment of this size and value.

One of the first things we did was to establish a clear division of responsibilities among our team. Govind would handle the logistics and ensure that the transportation of the gold from Uganda to Dubai went according to plan. Ram Kishan would be responsible for handling the quality assessments and building relationships with potential buyers in Dubai, ensuring we got the best possible deal for our gold. My role was to stay in Uganda and work directly with Jhon, Mr. Patrick, and the other members of the Gold Soko Africa Ltd team. I was the point of contact on the ground, overseeing every step and making sure everything was running smoothly.

Our first major hurdle was to make sure that all the documentation was in order. Ms. Achieng, the head of logistics and export at Gold Soko Africa Ltd, played a critical role in this process. She was meticulous, and her attention to detail was exactly what we needed. Together, we went through every piece of paperwork, ensuring that we had the necessary export licenses, certificates of origin, packing lists, and airway bills. Ms. Achieng was an expert at navigating the complex regulatory landscape, and her experience was invaluable in making sure our shipment would meet all the requirements for export.

The documentation process was extensive and time-consuming, but we couldn't afford to cut any corners. We spent countless hours checking and rechecking the paperwork, making sure that everything was in order. Ms. Achieng arranged meetings with customs officials to review the documentation and address any questions or concerns they might have. She emphasized the importance of building strong relationships with these officials, as they played a crucial role in ensuring that our shipment would pass smoothly through the customs process.

While the documentation was being finalized, I continued to work closely with Mr. Okello, the head of refining, to prepare the gold for shipment. The refining process was already complete, but there were still several steps we needed to take to ensure that the gold was ready for export. Each bar had to be carefully weighed and cataloged, with detailed records of its weight, purity, and origin. These records were crucial, as they would be used to verify the gold's authenticity at every stage of the journey.

Mr. Okello also conducted additional purity tests on the gold bars to verify that they met the required standards. He explained that these tests were not just for the benefit of the buyers, but also for the refinery itself. "If there is any discrepancy in the quality of the gold," he said, "it reflects poorly on us. We take great pride in maintaining our standards, and we want to ensure that our reputation remains untarnished." His dedication to quality was evident, and it gave me confidence that we were dealing with the best possible product.

Once the gold was prepared and all the necessary documentation was in place, we began to plan the logistics of transporting the gold to the airport. This was a critical step, as transporting a large quantity of gold was inherently risky. We needed to make sure that the gold was secure at all times, and that we had the right measures in place to prevent any potential issues during transit.

Ms. Achieng coordinated with a security company to arrange for armed guards to accompany the shipment from the refinery to Entebbe International Airport. The guards were experienced in handling high-value shipments, and they had a detailed plan for every aspect of the journey. The gold would be transported in a reinforced vehicle, and the route would be carefully planned to avoid any potential security risks. The guards would remain with the shipment until it was safely handed over to the airline for transport to Dubai.

The day of the shipment was one of the most nerve-racking experiences of my life. The refinery was abuzz with activity as everyone worked to make sure that everything was ready. The gold bars were carefully packed into secure crates, each one sealed and marked with its corresponding documentation. The guards arrived early, conducting a thorough check of the premises and going over the transport plan one final time. I could feel the tension in the air, but there was also a sense of excitement. This was the culmination of months of planning and hard work, and we were finally ready to take the next step.

As the gold was loaded into the transport vehicle, I couldn't help but feel a mix of emotions. There was excitement, of course—the thrill of seeing our plans come to fruition. But there was also a sense of anxiety. This was a significant undertaking, and there were so many factors that could go wrong. We were dealing with a highly valuable shipment, and we had to rely on the expertise and integrity of everyone involved to ensure that it reached its destination safely.

The journey to the airport was tense, but everything went according to plan. The guards remained vigilant, keeping a close eye on the vehicle and communicating with each other throughout the journey. We arrived at Entebbe International Airport without any issues, and the gold was handed over to the airline for transport to Dubai. Ms. Achieng had already coordinated with the airline and customs officials, and the shipment was cleared for departure without any delays. Watching the gold being loaded onto the plane, I felt a sense of relief. The first major step was complete, and now it was up to Govind and Ram Kishan to handle the rest in Dubai.

Once the gold was on its way, I stayed in close contact with Govind, who was waiting for the shipment in Dubai. He kept me updated on the progress of the flight and the preparations on their end. The plan was for the gold to be transported directly to a refinery in Dubai, where it would be tested again to verify its quality before being handed over to the buyer. Govind had already arranged for the necessary security and transport, and he assured me that everything was ready.

Meanwhile, Ram Kishan was busy working with potential buyers. He had reached out to several contacts in the Dubai gold market, and there was significant interest in our shipment. The competitive price we were offering, combined with the high purity of the gold, made it an attractive proposition for buyers. Ram Kishan's experience and reputation in the gold market were invaluable, and I knew that we were in good hands with him handling the negotiations.

While Govind and Ram Kishan were working on their end, I remained in Uganda, continuing to work closely with Jhon and Mr. Patrick. We knew that the success of our first shipment would determine the future of our venture, and we were already thinking ahead to the next steps. Mr. Patrick was optimistic, and he spoke about expanding our operations, sourcing larger quantities of gold, and building long-term relationships with buyers in Dubai and other markets. He believed that we had the potential to become a major player in the gold trade, and I was beginning to share his vision.

A few days after the shipment left Uganda, I received a call from Govind. The gold had arrived in Dubai safely, and it had passed all the necessary tests at the refinery. The buyer was satisfied with the quality, and we were ready to finalize the sale. Hearing this news was an incredible relief. The months of planning, the countless hours spent preparing, and the risks we had taken had all paid off. We had successfully completed our first shipment, and the profits we were set to make were substantial.

Ram Kishan handled the negotiations with the buyer, and within a few days, the deal was finalized. The buyer agreed to purchase the gold at a price of $29,500 per kilogram, giving us a significant profit margin of $5,500 per kilogram, resulting in a total profit of $137,500. The funds were transferred to our account, and just like that, our first major venture was complete. The sense of accomplishment I felt was overwhelming. We had faced numerous challenges, but we had overcome them and succeeded in our goal.

With the first shipment successfully completed, we began to plan for the future.

The success of the trial run had proven that our business model was viable, and we were eager to scale up our operations. We began to discuss the possibility of increasing the size of our next shipment, sourcing more gold from our partners in the DRC Congo, and expanding our network of buyers. There was still much work to be done, but we were ready to take on the challenge.

The experience of planning and executing our first shipment taught me many valuable lessons. I learned the importance of attention to detail, the need for meticulous planning, and the value of building strong relationships with the people involved in every aspect of the business. I also learned that in the gold trade, trust was everything. We had placed our trust in Jhon, Mr. Patrick, Ms. Achieng, and the many others who had helped us along the way, and they had delivered on their promises. It was a reminder that while the gold trade was a complex and challenging business, it was also one that could be immensely rewarding if approached with care and integrity.

As we moved forward, I knew that there would be new challenges and new risks. The gold trade was not for the faint of heart, and there were many factors beyond our control that could impact our success. But with the knowledge, experience, and partnerships we had built, I felt confident that we were on the right path. The journey ahead would not be easy, but it was a journey I was ready to take, one step at a time, toward a brighter future for all of us.

Chapter 8

The Initial Delays and Extra Fees

The success of our first shipment had given us the confidence to proceed with our plans. We were eager to scale up, to take advantage of the opportunities we saw in the gold trade. However, we were also aware that the gold business was unpredictable and that challenges could arise at any time. Despite our careful planning and meticulous preparation, the next chapter of our journey would prove to be far more challenging than we had anticipated.

After completing the first shipment, we began to prepare for the next one, which was planned to be significantly larger at 150 kilograms of 96% pure, 22-carat gold. The purchase price was \$24,000 per kilogram, while the market price ranged from \$29,500 to \$30,500 per kilogram. We paid a 7% advance payment of \$252,000 to cover initial costs. We were in high spirits, optimistic that we could capitalize on the momentum we had built. However, as we moved forward, we began to face a series of unexpected delays and complications that tested our resolve and forced us to rethink our approach.

The first challenge we faced was related to sourcing a larger quantity of gold. Our original partners in the DRC Congo had been reliable, but as we started negotiating for a larger shipment, we ran into obstacles. The miners, who had previously been eager to work with us, now seemed hesitant. They mentioned new difficulties in obtaining permits for transporting gold across the border into Uganda. The political situation in the DRC Congo was becoming more unstable, and the increased scrutiny from local authorities was making it more difficult for them to operate.

The uncertainty surrounding the supply of gold was unsettling. We had already secured buyers in Dubai who were interested in purchasing a larger quantity of gold, and they were expecting us to deliver on our promises. We needed to find a way to overcome the challenges in the DRC Congo or risk losing the trust of our buyers. I worked closely with Mr. Patrick to try and find a solution. We explored alternative sources of gold, reaching out to other mining operations in Uganda and even considering sourcing from neighboring countries. However, each potential solution came with its own set of challenges, and it was clear that we were facing an uphill battle.

While we were struggling to secure the gold, we were also facing new challenges on the logistical front. The success of our first shipment had attracted attention, and now we were facing increased scrutiny from the Ugandan authorities. Customs officials, who had previously been cooperative, were now raising questions about our operations. They wanted more documentation, more proof of the legitimacy of our supply chain, and more assurances that we were complying with all the necessary regulations. It felt like every step forward was met with new obstacles, and it was becoming increasingly difficult to keep up with the demands being placed on us.

Ms. Achieng, who had been instrumental in helping us navigate the customs process during our first shipment, was now spending most of her time dealing with government officials. She was meeting with them regularly, providing them with the information they requested, and trying to reassure them that we were operating above board. However, it was clear that something had changed. The process that had gone so smoothly the first time around was now fraught with delays and complications. It was frustrating, and it felt like we were being targeted for reasons beyond our control.

The delays in securing the gold and the challenges with customs were putting a strain on our partnership. Govind, who was in Dubai preparing for the next shipment, was growing increasingly concerned. He had buyers lined up, but without the gold, there was nothing to sell. He called me frequently, asking for updates and trying to understand what was causing the delays. I did my best to keep him informed, but the truth was that I didn't have all the answers. We were doing everything we could, but it felt like we were fighting an uphill battle.

Ram Kishan, too, was feeling the pressure. He had built relationships with buyers in Dubai who were eager to work with us, but the delays were beginning to erode their confidence. He was spending more and more time trying to reassure them, to keep them interested, but he could only do so much. The buyers wanted results, and we were struggling to deliver. The pressure was mounting, and it was clear that we needed to find a solution, and fast.

In the midst of all these challenges, Jhon remained a constant source of encouragement. He understood the difficulties we were facing, and he was always there to offer support and advice. He spoke about the ups and downs of the gold trade, the unpredictable nature of the business, and the importance of perseverance. "This is part of the journey," he would say. "There will always be challenges, but if we stay focused, we'll find a way through." His words were reassuring, but the reality of our situation was becoming increasingly difficult to ignore.

One of the most challenging aspects of this period was dealing with the uncertainty. We were used to having control, to being able to plan and execute with precision. But now, it felt like everything was out of our hands. We couldn't control the political situation in the DRC Congo, we couldn't control the actions of the customs officials, and we couldn't control the expectations of our buyers. All we could do was adapt, to try and find a way forward despite the obstacles in our path.

In an effort to address the challenges we were facing, Mr. Patrick and I decided to travel to the DRC Congo to meet with our mining partners in person. We wanted to understand what was causing the delays and see if there was anything we could do to help. The journey was long and arduous, and it gave me a firsthand look at the challenges the miners were facing. The situation on the ground was far more complicated than I had realized. The local authorities were cracking down on mining operations, demanding additional permits and imposing new restrictions. The miners were frustrated, and many of them were considering abandoning their operations altogether.

Despite the challenges, we managed to secure a commitment from one of our partners to provide the gold we needed for our next shipment. It wasn't as much as we had initially planned, but it was enough to move forward. We returned to Uganda with a renewed sense of determination, ready to do whatever it took to get our venture back on track.

Back in Uganda, we faced another hurdle. The customs officials, who had been questioning our operations, were now demanding additional inspections and certifications before they would allow the gold to be exported. It was clear that they were looking for any reason to delay the shipment, and it felt like we were being singled out. Ms. Achieng was working tirelessly to meet their demands, but it was a slow and frustrating process. We had to bring in additional experts to conduct the inspections, and each new requirement added more time and cost to the operation.

The delays were taking a toll on all of us. Govind was growing increasingly frustrated, and Ram Kishan was struggling to keep the buyers in Dubai on board. The uncertainty was affecting our relationships, and it was clear that we needed to find a way to regain control of the situation. We held several meetings to discuss our options, and it was during one of these meetings that we made a difficult decision. Given the challenges we were facing in Uganda, we decided to explore the possibility of moving our operations to Kenya. We had heard that the customs process in Kenya was more straightforward, and we hoped that relocating would help us avoid some of the obstacles we were facing.

The decision to move our operations was not an easy one. We had built relationships in Uganda, and we had invested a significant amount of time and resources into setting up our operations there. But it was clear that the situation was becoming untenable, and we needed to find a way to move forward. Fortunately, Mr. Patrick already had an office, refinery, storage facilities, and a team in place in Kenya. This setup made the move easier, though it soon became apparent that Mr. Patrick had planned this move to leverage additional control over the operation.

The move to Kenya was a major undertaking. We had to transport the gold across the border, as the rest of the equipment and infrastructure were already available in Kenya, thanks to Mr. Patrick's setup. It was a complex process, and there were moments when it felt like we were in over our heads. But we were determined to make it work. We coordinated with our partners, hired additional security, and made the journey to Nairobi, where we hoped to find a more favorable environment for our business.

Arriving in Nairobi, we were met with a mix of hope and uncertainty. The city was bustling, full of opportunity, but we knew that we still had a long road ahead of us. It was here that Mr. Patrick revealed his plan. He had already set up an office, a refinery, storage facilities, and a team to handle customs and logistics. His staff in Kenya had already established strong relationships with the customs officers, which allowed them to navigate the bureaucratic processes more effectively. Everything was in place, but it became evident that his intention was to leverage this setup to demand more from us.

Mr. Patrick requested an additional 9.5% of the invoice amount, which amounted to $342,000, claiming it was necessary for covering the costs associated with customs and other formalities in Kenya. It was clear that he had planned this move all along, setting up the infrastructure in Kenya to exert more control and extract additional funds from us. Despite our frustration, we had no choice but to comply if we wanted to keep the venture moving forward.

The initial days in Nairobi were challenging. We were working around the clock, trying to set up our operations and get everything in order.

Chapter 9

The Scam

The reality of our situation started to unravel slowly, like a carefully woven thread coming undone. Despite the challenges we had faced and overcome, we were still hopeful that everything would work out as planned. We had faced delays, additional fees, and logistical headaches, but we were determined to see the venture through to success. The move to Kenya had seemed like a new beginning, a chance to start fresh and leave the problems in Uganda behind. But little did we know, this was the beginning of the end.

The first sign that something was wrong came when we received word that the gold shipment we had worked so hard to prepare had not arrived in Dubai as scheduled. Govind, who had been anxiously waiting for the shipment, called me in a panic. He had everything prepared—buyers lined up, documents in place, and security on standby—but there was no sign of the shipment. At first, we assumed it was just another delay, perhaps an issue with customs or a minor logistical hiccup. But as hours turned into days, it became clear that this was no ordinary delay.

I immediately reached out to Mr. Patrick for an explanation. He had always been our main point of contact, the person who had assured us time and time again that everything was under control. But now, my calls went unanswered. My messages were ignored. The sense of unease that had been building over the past few weeks began to grow into something more—an unsettling realization that we were being deceived. I tried contacting Jhon as well, hoping that he could shed some light on the situation, but he too was unreachable.

With no response from either Mr. Patrick or Jhon, and with the Kenya office staff refusing to provide any information about the shipment, I decided to return to Kampala to find out what was going on. When I arrived at Mr. Patrick's office in Kampala, I was met with yet another obstacle. The security guard at the entrance refused to let me in, saying that Mr. Patrick was not available and that I wasn't allowed to enter. It was at that moment that I realized just how deeply I had been deceived and how far they were willing to go to keep me in the dark.

The more I tried to get answers, the more elusive they became. The office in Nairobi, which had been bustling with activity just days before, was now eerily quiet. The staff who had once greeted me warmly now avoided eye contact, and Mr. Patrick was nowhere to be found. I visited the office several times, hoping to catch him there, but each time I was met with excuses—"He's out on business,", "He's in a meeting,", "He just stepped out." It was clear that they were stalling, trying to keep me at bay while they figured out their next move.

It was during one of these visits that the harsh reality finally hit me. I overheard a conversation between two staff members, speaking in hushed tones about the "plan" and how everything was "falling apart." My heart sank as I realized that this wasn't just a series of unfortunate events—this was a well-orchestrated scam. Everything—the delays, the additional fees, the move to Kenya—had been part of a carefully crafted plan to extract as much money from us as possible before disappearing without a trace.

The sense of betrayal was overwhelming. I had trusted these people. I had believed in the vision they had painted, the promises they had made. I had put everything on the line—my time, my money, my reputation—all for a venture that had turned out to be nothing more than a lie. The trust I had placed in Mr. Patrick, in Jhon, in the entire operation, had been shattered. The people who had once called me their "brother" had betrayed me in the worst possible way.

The most terrifying moment came one evening when there was a loud knock at the door of my hotel room. I opened the door to find ten men standing there—some of them I recognized from the office, others were strangers. Before I could react, they barged into my room, demanding that I hand over my passport, mobile phone, laptop, and wallet. They took everything from me, including all my identification and money. One of them looked into my eyes and said, "If you don't stop what you're doing, we will kill you." So stop chasing unnecessarily; you will get nothing. The threat was real, and the fear that gripped me in that moment was unlike anything I had ever experienced.

At that moment, the world around me felt empty and hollow. I felt a sudden shock like a heavy weight crushing my chest, making it hard to breathe. Time seemed to stand still, and all I could feel was deafening silence. My mind went blank, unable to process the enormity of what had just happened.

They left me in the room, stripped of everything that could help me. I had no money, no way to contact anyone, and no way to leave the country. I was trapped. The days that followed were some of the darkest I had ever experienced. I was stuck in that hotel room, unable to pay my bills, unable to leave, and with no way to reach out for help. I survived on the bare minimum—500 ml of water and two pieces of bread with two eggs a day. I had no money for food, and each day felt like an eternity. I lost weight, I lost hope, and I began to feel like I was slowly fading away. I stayed in that hotel room for 27 days, with no money, no food, and no way out. There were moments when I felt like giving up, moments when the thought of dying seemed like an escape from the nightmare I was living. Endless suicidal thoughts were bursting in my head.

It was during this time that the hotel staff began to notice my condition. The housekeeping staff would come to clean my room and noticed that I wasn't eating, that I wasn't leaving the room, that I wasn't paying my bills. Eventually, the hotel manager came to see me. He asked me what was happening, and I broke down, telling him everything. I told him about the scam, about how I had lost everything, and about how I had been threatened. He listened, and for the first time in weeks, I felt like someone cared for me. During that time when we were discussing my unfortunate situation, I was about to cry, somehow I managed myself and gathered the remaining strength to initiate further talk. We were in deep conversation but suddenly the hotel manager looked at me with an intense sulking face, for a while, I got scared but then the hotel manager asked me a question, "You are still alive? How…?"

I had no answer for his question, and I remained silent for a while. But at the same time, I got to know that it is the biggest miracle that happened in my life as I have survived for almost a month in the worst scenario without food, money, and loved ones.

The hotel manager, a kind man named Samuel, decided to help me. He offered me a room in his own house so that I could leave the hotel without having to worry about the mounting bill. He also gave me a second-hand mobile phone so that I could try to contact someone for help. With his assistance, I managed to get in touch with one of my cousins back in India. I explained my situation, and he agreed to send me some money—enough to pay off the hotel bill and give me a little to survive on.

Samuel also introduced me to his girlfriend, who was a lawyer working at the Ugandan High Court. She listened to my story and understood the gravity of my situation. She told me that if I tried to pursue the matter legally, I would face a lengthy process, and without the proper documentation or a work permit, I could even end up in jail. Instead, she offered to help me to negotiate with Mr. Patrick to get my passport back. I have shared all the required information to set up their communication, as I found a ray of hope to live again. It took almost three months of back-and-forth negotiations, but eventually, she managed to convince Mr. Patrick to return my passport. When I finally held it in my hands, it felt like a small victory in the midst of a crushing defeat.

But my troubles were far from over. My visa had expired during the time I was stuck in the hotel, and I was now facing fines for overstaying in Uganda. Each day of overstay came with a hefty fine, and I had no way to pay it. Samuel's girlfriend once again stepped in to help. She found someone who worked with the Ugandan immigration department and who was willing to help me get my passport stamped with a visa extension from the DRC Congo border. It wasn't entirely legal, but it was my only way out. We paid him, and after five days, he returned my passport, stamped and ready for me to leave the country. I was unable to thank Samuel and his girlfriend enough. I wanted to show my gratitude for what they had done for me but I had no other option rather than to choose words over anything. I thanked them and wished them a very happy life. After the interaction with Samuel and his girlfriend, I came to know that "humanity is still alive". A blissful, prudent, and benevolent soul can save someone from a near-death experience.

With my passport in hand, I was finally able to leave Uganda. Samuel, ever the kind soul, booked me a bus ticket from Kampala to Nairobi, where I could stay with one of his relatives until I could figure out what to do next. I arrived in Nairobi, exhausted and broken, but determined to keep fighting. I had lost everything—my money, my business, my trust in people—but I was still alive, and as long as I was alive, I had a chance to rebuild.

In Nairobi, I began to make efforts to raise awareness about gold scams. I created a fake Facebook account and started writing articles about my experience. I joined WhatsApp groups for traders and shared my story, hoping that it would prevent others from making the same mistakes I had made. Over time, I managed to help more than 150 people avoid falling victim to similar scams. It wasn't much, but it gave me a sense of purpose, a reason to keep going.

The sense of betrayal and loss was immense, but encircled by the darkness, there was also a glimmer of hope. I realized that I could use my experience to help others, to raise awareness about the dangers of gold scams, and to prevent others from making the same mistakes I had made. It wasn't the outcome I had hoped for, but it was a way to turn my pain into something meaningful, to find some sense of purpose in the midst of the chaos.

I began documenting everything I had experienced—the meetings, the promises, the documents, the payments. I wanted to create a record, not just for myself, but for others who might find themselves in a similar situation. I reached out to fellow traders who were in contact with gold dealers in Africa, sharing my experience and warning them about the scams.

I spoke to people in the industry and realized that scams like the one I had experienced were far more common than I had imagined.

The more I shared my story, the more I began to hear from others who had similar experiences. Traders from different parts of the world reached out to me, sharing their own tales of betrayal and loss. Some had been scammed by the same people—Mr. Patrick, Jhon, and their associates—while others had fallen victim to similar networks operating in other parts of Africa. The details varied, but the core of the scam was always the same: gaining trust, making grand promises, and then disappearing once the money had been paid.

These conversations were both heartbreaking and empowering. On one hand, it was devastating to realize just how many people had suffered the same fate as I had. On the other hand, it gave me a sense of community, a sense that I was not alone in my struggle. We began to exchange information, to connect the dots between different scammers and their operations. Slowly, a clearer picture of the network began to emerge, and I realized that these scams were far more organized and widespread than I had initially thought.

In Nairobi, I also took on whatever work I could find to sustain myself. I worked odd jobs, anything that would pay enough to cover my basic needs. The money wasn't much, but it was enough to keep me going. I knew that if I wanted to rebuild my life, I would have to start from the ground up, and I was willing to do whatever it took. My focus was on survival, on staying strong, and on finding a way to move forward.

The days were long and often filled with uncertainty, but I refused to give up. Each morning, I would remind myself that I had survived the worst, so I cannot miss that last opportunity to regain my lost existence.

Chapter 10

The Nairobi Move

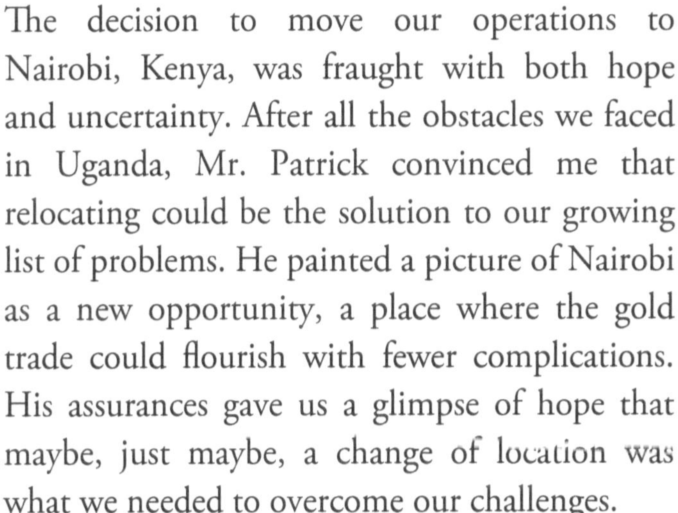

The decision to move our operations to Nairobi, Kenya, was fraught with both hope and uncertainty. After all the obstacles we faced in Uganda, Mr. Patrick convinced me that relocating could be the solution to our growing list of problems. He painted a picture of Nairobi as a new opportunity, a place where the gold trade could flourish with fewer complications. His assurances gave us a glimpse of hope that maybe, just maybe, a change of location was what we needed to overcome our challenges.

Mr. Patrick claimed to have all the necessary connections in Kenya—contacts in customs, secure storage facilities, and a trusted team. According to him, Nairobi would be a place where the authorities would be easier to navigate, where the logistics would work smoothly, and where the barriers we had faced in Uganda would be eliminated. At that point, I was desperate to find a solution, and the hope of a fresh start was enough to make me agree to the move. I had no idea at the time that it would lead to even more complications and frustrations.

The logistics of the move were overwhelming. Transporting gold across the border was a risky and complicated endeavor. Despite Mr. Patrick's claims that everything was arranged, I couldn't help but feel uneasy. We hired security, organized transport, and managed the paperwork needed to cross the border. It was a tense journey, but I convinced myself that this was just another hurdle that needed to be overcome. I held onto the hope that things would get better once we got to Nairobi.

Upon arrival, I felt a renewed sense of optimism. Nairobi was a bustling city, filled with energy and opportunity. Mr. Patrick took me to see the office he had set up, complete with a refinery and storage facilities. He introduced me to his Kenyan team, and they seemed capable and professional. For a brief moment, I allowed myself to believe that the worst was behind us, that this move might actually be the key to our success.

However, the optimism was short-lived. The problems started almost immediately. Within days, Mr. Patrick informed me of unexpected expenses that we had not accounted for. He claimed that the Kenyan authorities were demanding extra money for customs clearance and documentation—an additional 9.5% of the invoice value, totaling $342,000. He insisted that these fees were essential to ensure smooth operations, but it felt like yet another way to siphon money from us. Despite my growing doubts, I felt I had no choice but to comply. We had already invested so much in this venture, and backing out was not an option.

The additional payments were just the beginning. Delays began to pile up, and Govind, who was in Dubai preparing for the shipment, was becoming increasingly frustrated. He had buyers lined up and was ready to receive the gold, but with no shipment, there was nothing to deliver. He called me frequently, seeking updates and trying to understand why things were taking so long. I did my best to reassure him, to tell him that progress was being made, but deep down, I was just as frustrated. Nairobi was supposed to be our fresh start, but it was quickly turning into another nightmare.

Despite the extra payments, it seemed that the Kenyan customs officials were never satisfied. There were always more documents to be provided, more inspections to be conducted, and more hurdles to jump through. It felt like we were being strung along with no end in sight. The hope that relocating to Nairobi would solve our problems was fading, replaced by the grim reality that we were facing the same obstacles as before—only now, we were dealing with new expenses and new challenges.

As the days turned into weeks, I started to see through the promises Mr. Patrick had made. The office, which at first seemed so well-organized, was disorganized behind the scenes. The refinery, which was supposed to be a key part of our operation, faced constant issues—

equipment malfunctions, processing delays, and questions about the gold's quality. The Kenyan staff, who had initially seemed competent, now appeared overwhelmed and poorly managed. It was becoming painfully clear that Mr. Patrick had oversold his Nairobi setup, and we were the ones paying the price for his lies.

The pressure from my partners was unrelenting. Govind and Ram Kishan had trusted me with their money and their faith, and I could sense that trust was beginning to erode. They had believed in the vision I had presented, and now they were starting to question whether they had made a terrible mistake. I was questioning it too. But I couldn't afford to show my doubts. I had to keep pushing forward, even though everything seemed to be unraveling around me.

There was one moment in particular that felt like a breaking point. We had finally managed to get the gold ready for shipment, and I thought we were finally going to move forward. But then, Mr. Patrick informed me that there were additional fees that needed to be paid—this time for security and transportation arrangements to ensure the gold reached Dubai safely. The amount was significant, and I felt like we were never going to reach the finish line. Every time we thought we were making progress, another obstacle would appear, another payment would be demanded. It was becoming clear that Mr. Patrick had no intention of ever letting us succeed. He was simply trying to extract as much money from us as possible before everything collapsed.

The frustration and sense of betrayal were becoming traumatic and unbearable. I had come to Nairobi with hopes of finally seeing our hard work pay off, but all I was seeing was more lies and deceit. The expenses were piling up, and we were running out of resources. Govind and Ram Kishan were losing faith in me, and I felt the weight of their disappointment. I had led them into this mess, and I felt responsible for the situation we were in. But I was beginning to realize that Mr. Patrick had been leading us on from the start, keeping us hooked with false promises and fabricated opportunities.

One day, after yet another demand for payment, I decided that enough was enough. I confronted Mr. Patrick directly, demanding answers. I asked him why there were always more fees, why we never seemed to make any real progress. He looked me in the eye and calmly told me that this was just the way the gold trade worked, that there were always unforeseen expenses and challenges. But I knew better by then. I could see that he was stalling, trying to keep us strung along for as long as possible. It was a painful realization, but it was also a moment of clarity. I knew then that I couldn't keep going down this path.

I began to consider my options. I knew that I had to find a way to cut our losses and walk away before it was too late. But it wasn't just my money on the line—Govind and Ram Kishan had invested in this venture, and I couldn't just abandon them. I felt a deep sense of responsibility to try and make things right. But as the days went by, it became increasingly clear that there was no salvaging this situation. The move to Nairobi, which I had once believed would be our saving grace, had turned out to be just another part of the elaborate scam.

The hardest part was accepting that we had been deceived from the very beginning. The hope that Nairobi would be different, that we could overcome the challenges we faced in Uganda, had been nothing more than an illusion. Mr. Patrick had used that hope to keep us invested, to keep us paying, while he never intended to deliver on any of his promises. The realization was crushing, but it was also liberating. It allowed me to see the situation for what it truly was—a dead end. And as much as it pained me, I knew that the only way forward was to cut ties and find a new path.

Looking back, the move to Nairobi was a pivotal moment. It was the point where I truly began to understand the depth of the deception, the lengths to which Mr. Patrick would go to keep us entangled in his web of lies. It was a painful lesson, but it was one that I needed to learn. It opened my eyes to the fact that we were never going to succeed as long as we were under Mr. Patrick's control. The dream of building a successful gold trading business had turned into a nightmare, and it was time to wake up and face reality. The hope that Nairobi might solve our problems had been an illusion, and it was time to let go and move forward on my own terms.

Chapter 11

The Missing Gold and The Ultimatum

The days following our supposed shipment from Nairobi were some of the most anxiety-ridden of my life. We had faced numerous obstacles along the way, but at least I thought we had finally reached a point where we could fulfill our commitment to our buyers in Dubai. The shipment was supposed to be on its way, and Govind was in Dubai, prepared to receive it. But as the days passed, there was no word of the gold's arrival, and it became increasingly clear that something had gone terribly wrong.

Govind called me, his voice full of worry and frustration. He had everything arranged—the buyers, the refineries, the security. The buyers, too, were growing restless, asking for updates, demanding to know why there was a delay. I tried to remain calm, hoping that it was just a minor logistical issue, that the shipment would arrive soon. But deep down, a feeling of dread was building. I couldn't deny the nagging suspicion that we had been deceived yet again.

I tried contacting Mr. Patrick, demanding an explanation for the delay. But just like before, he was nowhere to be found. My calls went unanswered, my messages ignored. I reached out to Jhon as well, hoping that he could shed some light on the situation, but he too had gone silent. The Nairobi office, which had been bustling with activity just days earlier, was now practically deserted. The staff who had once welcomed me with open arms now avoided me, their eyes downcast, their expressions unreadable.

The pressure from Govind and Ram Kishan was relentless. They had put their trust in me, invested their money and their faith, and now they were watching everything fall apart. Govind's calls became more frequent, his voice increasingly tense. He demanded answers that I couldn't provide. He wanted to know where the gold was, why it hadn't arrived, and what we were going to do about it. Each time I spoke to him, I could feel the weight of his disappointment and anger. I had promised him that this venture would be a success, and now it seemed like all those promises were turning into dust.

As the situation grew more dire, I made the difficult decision to return to Kampala to confront Mr. Patrick in person. I had to find out what had happened to the shipment. I had to get answers, not just for myself, but for Govind and Ram Kishan as well. When I arrived at Mr. Patrick's office in Kampala, I was met by a security guard who refused to let me in. He claimed that Mr. Patrick wasn't available and that I had no right to enter. I insisted, trying to push my way past him, but he stood firm. It was clear that I wasn't going to get anywhere. I was left standing outside the office, the realization slowly sinking in that I had been shut out completely.

The sense of helplessness was overwhelming. I had come so far, put everything I had into this venture, and now I was standing outside a locked door, unable to get answers, unable to move forward. It was becoming increasingly clear that Mr. Patrick had no intention of ever delivering on his promises. The move to Nairobi, the assurances of smooth operations, the promises of success—they had all been lies. Lies designed to keep us hooked, to keep us paying, while Mr. Patrick and his associates drained us of every last resource.

Back in Nairobi, I tried to gather whatever information I could. I spoke to the few staff members who were still around, but they either didn't know anything or were too afraid to talk. It was as if a veil had been drawn over the entire operation, and I was left in the dark, grasping at straws. The frustration and anxiety were eating away at me. I couldn't sleep, couldn't think clearly. All I could think about was the missing gold, the money we had invested, and the buyers in Dubai who were waiting for something that would never arrive.

The pressure from Govind and Ram Kishan reached a breaking point. They were furious, demanding that I take action, that I find a way to recover the gold or at least the money we had invested. They were no longer willing to wait, no longer willing to trust in Mr. Patrick's empty promises. They gave me an ultimatum: either find a way to resolve the situation or face the consequences. The consequences were clear— they would hold me personally responsible for the losses, and they would take whatever steps were necessary to recover their money.

I felt trapped, cornered by circumstances that were spiraling out of control. I had no idea how to resolve the situation, no idea where to even begin looking for the missing gold. It was as if the ground had been ripped out from under me, and I was left floundering, struggling to find something to hold onto. I knew that I couldn't give up, that I had to keep fighting, but I also knew that I was running out of options.

In a last-ditch effort, I decided to reach out to some of the other contacts I had made during my time in Nairobi. I spoke to traders, transporters, anyone who might have heard something about the missing shipment. I spent days visiting different offices, making phone calls, trying to piece together the puzzle. But every lead I followed turned out to be a dead end. It was as if the gold had simply vanished, leaving no trace behind.

The mounting anxiety was devastating. I couldn't eat, couldn't sleep, couldn't escape the constant feeling of dread. Every day felt like a waking nightmare, a constant reminder of everything that had gone wrong. I thought about all the sacrifices I had made, all the risks I had taken, and it felt like it had all been for nothing. The realization that we had been scammed was becoming impossible to ignore, but I still clung to a sliver of hope that somehow, there was a way out.

One evening, as I sat alone in my hotel room, I received a call from Govind. His voice was cold, devoid of any of the warmth or camaraderie we had once shared. He told me that he could no longer wait, that he had lost faith in the venture, and that he wanted his money back. He didn't care how I got it—he just wanted it back. The conversation left me feeling hollow, the weight of his words crushing me. I had lost not only the gold and the money but also the trust of my partners and friends.

I knew then that I had reached a crossroads. I could continue to chase after the missing gold, continue to believe in Mr. Patrick's lies, or I could face the truth and start thinking about how to move forward. It was a painful decision, but it was one that I knew I had to make. The gold was gone, and with it, all the dreams and hopes I had built around this venture. I had to accept the reality of the situation and start thinking about how to rebuild, how to make things right for Govind and Ram Kishan, and how to move on from the nightmare that had consumed my life.

The days that followed were some of the hardest I had ever faced. I had to confront my partners, to tell them the truth, to accept responsibility for what had happened. It was humiliating, painful, and it felt like I was losing everything I had worked for. But it was also a turning point. For the first time in a long time, I stopped chasing after false promises and started focusing on what I could do to make things right. The gold was gone, but I was still here, and as long as I was alive, there was a chance to rebuild, to start over, and to learn from the mistakes that had brought me to this point.

Looking back, the missing shipment was the final straw, the moment when everything came crashing down. It was the culmination of all the lies, all the deceit, all the false hope that had kept me going. It was a painful lesson, but it was also a necessary one. It forced me to confront the reality of the situation, to let go of the illusions I had clung to, and to start thinking about how to move forward on my own terms. The gold may have been lost, but I was determined not to let it define me. I was ready to face whatever came next, to rebuild from the ashes, and to find a way to move forward despite everything that had gone wrong.

Chapter 12

The Fight for Survival

After the realization that the gold was gone and that all the promises had been nothing more than deceit, my life in Kampala took a dark turn. The threats, the loss, and the growing sense of helplessness culminated in a moment that I will never forget—the night a group of men forced their way into my hotel room, robbed me of everything I had, and left me fearing for my life.

One evening when I heard the knock at the door. At first, I thought it was just a member of the hotel staff, but when I opened the door, I was met by ten men—some of whom I recognized from Mr. Patrick's office. They pushed their way in, their expressions cold and menacing. Before I knew what was happening, they demanded that I hand over my passport, my mobile phone, my laptop, and my wallet. They left no room for negotiation. One of them grabbed me by the collar and hissed, "If you don't stop what you're doing, we will kill you." The words sent a shiver down my spine. It was the most direct threat I had ever faced, and in that moment, I felt a deep sense of vulnerability. I was alone in a foreign country, with no one to turn to and no way to protect myself.

After they took everything, I was left in my room, completely stripped of anything that could help me. My passport, my money, my phone— all gone. I had no way to contact anyone, no way to leave the country, and no way to pay my mounting hotel bills. I was stuck, trapped in that room, and the fear that those men would come back haunted me day and night. I couldn't sleep, couldn't eat, couldn't think of anything but the threat that hung over me. Every sound in the hallway made me jump, every knock on the door sent my heart racing.

"Fear is a slow poison," and this slow poison has forced me to experience a slow death.

The days that followed were some of the darkest I had ever experienced. I was isolated in that small hotel room, unable to leave, unable to pay for food or basic necessities. I survived on the bare minimum—a small bottle of water, a couple of pieces of bread, and whatever scraps I could get my hands on. The hotel staff, who had once been friendly and welcoming, now looked at me with a mixture of pity and suspicion. They knew I couldn't pay my bills, and I could see their patience wearing thin. I had no money, no support, and no idea how I was going to get out of this situation.

It was during this time that I began to lose hope. I had fought so hard to make this venture work, had sacrificed so much, and now I was at rock bottom. I felt like a prisoner, trapped in that room, with no way out. I thought about my family back home, about the people who had trusted me, and I felt a deep sense of shame. I had failed them, and I had failed myself. There were moments when I thought about giving up entirely, moments when the thought of escaping the pain seemed like the only option. But something inside me refused to let go, refused to give in to the darkness.

One morning, after almost a month of barely surviving, the hotel manager came to my room. He had noticed that I wasn't eating, that I wasn't leaving the room, that I was in desperate need of help. He asked me what was going on, and for the first time, I broke down. I told him everything—the scam, the threats, the loss of my passport, and the fact that I had no money to pay for anything. He listened quietly, his expression softening as I spoke. When I finished, he nodded and said, "You need help, and I'm going to do what I can to help you."

The hotel manager, Samuel, was a kind man. He offered me a lifeline when I needed it most. He told me that I could stay at his house until I figured out what to do. He also gave me a second-hand mobile phone so I could try to contact someone for help. His kindness brought tears to my eyes. After everything I had been through, after all the lies and betrayals, here was someone who was willing to help me without asking for anything in return. It was a small glimmer of hope in an otherwise hopeless situation.

With the phone Samuel gave me, I managed to contact one of my cousins back in India. I explained my situation, and he agreed to send me some money—enough to pay off my hotel bill and give me a little to survive on. When the money finally arrived, I paid what I owed to the hotel and moved in with Samuel. His house was modest, but it was a sanctuary compared to the hotel room that had begun to feel like a prison. For the first time in weeks, I felt a sense of safety, a sense that maybe, just maybe, things could get better.

Samuel's girlfriend was also a source of support. She worked as a lawyer at the Ugandan High Court, and when she heard about my situation, she offered to help me get my passport back. She told me that pursuing the matter legally would be difficult, especially since I had no work permit or proper documentation. But she was determined to help me, and she began negotiating with Mr. Patrick and his associates to return my passport. It was a long and arduous process, filled with setbacks and delays, but eventually, her persistence paid off. After three months of negotiations, I finally had my passport in my hands again. It was a small victory, but it felt like a turning point. It was a sign that I still had a chance to make it out of this nightmare.

However, my problems were far from over. My visa had expired during the time I was trapped in the hotel, and I was now facing fines for overstaying in Uganda. Each day of overstay came with a hefty fine, and I had no way to pay it. Samuel's girlfriend once again stepped in to help. She found someone who worked with the Ugandan immigration department who was willing to help me get my passport stamped with a visa extension from the DRC Congo border. It wasn't entirely legal, but it was my only way out. We paid him, and after five days, he returned my passport, stamped and ready for me to leave the country.

With my passport finally in order, Samuel helped me book a bus ticket from Kampala to Nairobi. He had a relative in Nairobi who was willing to let me stay with them until I could figure out my next steps. The journey to Nairobi was long and exhausting, but as I crossed the border, I felt a sense of relief. I was leaving behind the place that had brought me so much pain and suffering, and I was ready to start over. I had lost everything—my money, my business, my trust in people—but I was still alive, and as long as I was alive, I had a chance to restart.

My time in Nairobi was not easy, but it was a new beginning. I started looking for work, taking whatever jobs I could find to make ends meet. I also began writing about my experiences, sharing my story on social media to warn others about the dangers of gold scams. It wasn't much, but it gave me a sense of purpose, a reason to keep going. Slowly but surely, I began to rebuild my life. The fight for survival in Kampala had taken everything from me, but it had also taught me something important—that no matter how dire the circumstances, no matter how hopeless things seemed, I could still find a way to keep going.

Looking back, my time in that Kampala hotel room was the darkest period of my life. The fear, the isolation, the constant threats—it all felt like too much to bear. But it was also a time of transformation. It stripped away everything I thought I knew about myself, about trust, about success, and forced me to confront who I truly was. It showed me the depths of my own resilience, my ability to survive even when everything seemed lost. And for that, I am grateful. The fight for survival wasn't just about staying alive—it was about finding a way to move forward, no matter how impossible it seemed.

Last but not the least, "I had conquered the slow poison." Fear is an inherent part of us; our response to it is what matters.

Chapter 13

The Cost of Returning Home

After months of fighting for survival in Kampala, I finally had my passport in hand, and it was time to think about returning to India. But the path home was not going to be easy. There were still many obstacles standing in my way, and the emotional and financial toll of the past months weighed heavily on me. I had lost everything—my business, my trust in people, and even my freedom to travel—and the struggle to leave Uganda would prove to be yet another test of my endurance.

My first hurdle was dealing with the visa fines. My visa had expired long ago, and for every day I had overstayed, there was a hefty fine. The total amount was staggering, and I had no idea how I was going to pay it. Samuel's girlfriend, who had helped me get my passport back, continued to assist me. She managed to find someone within the Ugandan immigration department who was willing to help me resolve the visa issue, albeit through unconventional means. It wasn't entirely legal, but it was my only chance to leave the country without facing jail time for the overstay. The immigration officer agreed to help me for a fee, and after days of anxious waiting, I finally had my passport stamped and ready for travel.

Even with my visa issue resolved, there was still the question of money. I had no funds left, and I needed money for transportation, food, and my journey back to India. With no other options, I made the difficult decision to sell my home in India. It was a painful choice—that house had been more than just a place to live; it was a symbol of everything I had worked for, the life I had built for myself and my family. But now, it was the only asset I had left, and I needed the money to repay Govind and Ram Kishan, my partners who had invested their trust and finances in me.

The process of selling my home was emotionally draining. I contacted my family and explained the situation. They were devastated, but they understood that there was no other option. My relative back in India helped to find a buyer, and within a few weeks, the house was sold. The money I received was enough to pay off the debts I owed to Govind and Ram Kishan, and with a heavy heart, I transferred the funds to them. It wasn't just about the money—it was about trying to make things right, to repay the people who had believed in me, even if I had failed to deliver on my promises.

Once the debts were repaid, I used what little money was left to arrange my journey back to India. Samuel, who had been a lifeline for me during my darkest days, helped me book a bus ticket from Kampala to Nairobi. From there, I would take a flight back to India. Saying goodbye to Samuel and his girlfriend was difficult. They had become like family to me, offering me shelter and support when I had nothing. I thanked them both, promising to stay in touch and never forgetting the kindness they had shown me.

The bus ride from Kampala to Nairobi was long and exhausting. As the miles passed, I couldn't help but think about everything that had happened over the past several months. The excitement of the initial opportunity, the trust I had placed in Mr. Patrick and Jhon, the move to Nairobi that was supposed to change everything—it had all led to heartbreak, loss, and betrayal. I had been naive, too trusting, and I had paid the price for it. But despite everything, I was still alive, and I was finally on my way home.

When I arrived in Nairobi, I had to wait for a few days before my flight back to India. I stayed with Samuel's relative, who had kindly agreed to take me in until my departure. During those few days, I spent my time reflecting on the journey I had been through. I thought about the people I had met along the way—some who had betrayed me, others who had helped me. I realized that despite the pain and the loss, there was still good in the world, and there were still people willing to lend a hand to a stranger in need.

The day of my flight finally arrived. As I boarded the plane, I felt a mix of emotions—relief, sadness, exhaustion, and even a glimmer of hope. I was leaving behind the nightmare that had consumed my life for so long, but I was also leaving behind the people who had saved me, who had given me a chance to start over. The flight back to India felt surreal, as if I was caught between two worlds—the life I had lost and the uncertain future that awaited me.

When I landed in India, I was overwhelmed with emotion. I was finally home, but everything had changed. I had lost my house, my business, and my financial stability. I had to start from scratch, rebuild everything I had lost, and try to find a way to move forward. The burden of the past weighed heavily on me, but I was determined to keep going. I knew that I couldn't change what had happened, but I could learn from it. I could use my experience to warn others, to help them avoid making the same mistakes I had made.

The first few weeks back in India were difficult. I had to find a place to live, find work, and begin the process of rebuilding my life. I started by reaching out to old contacts, trying to revive my garment and footwear business. It wasn't easy—I had lost my reputation, and many people were hesitant to work with me again. But I refused to give up. Slowly, I began to regain the trust of my clients, to rebuild the business that I had once lost.

The financial toll of my experience in Uganda was immense, but the emotional toll was even greater. I had lost friends, faced threats, and endured months of isolation and fear. I had to confront my own failures, to accept responsibility for the choices I had made. But in the end, I also found strength I didn't know I had. I had survived the worst, and I was still standing. I had faced betrayal, loss, and despair, but I had also found kindness, resilience, and the will to keep fighting.

Looking back, the cost of returning home was more than just financial. It was the cost of lost dreams, lost trust, and lost time. But it was also the beginning of a new chapter. A chapter where I could use my experiences to help others, to raise awareness about the dangers of gold scams, and to rebuild my life on my own terms. The journey was far from over, but I was ready to face whatever came next, armed with the lessons I had learned and the resilience I had gained.

Chapter 14

Awareness as a Mission

After returning to India, I knew that I couldn't let my experience be in vain. I had faced betrayal, threats, and unimaginable hardship, and I knew that there were others out there who could easily fall into the same trap. The thought of others experiencing the same pain and loss drove me to take action. I decided to dedicate myself to raising awareness about the dangers of gold scams. It became my mission to help others avoid the mistakes I had made, and to use my story as a warning to anyone considering getting involved in such ventures.

Social media became my primary tool for spreading the message. I created profiles on various platforms, sharing my story in detail, outlining the tactics scammers used, and providing practical advice on how to identify and avoid fraudulent schemes. It wasn't easy at first—reliving the experience, talking about my failures and the mistakes I had made. But I knew it was necessary. If my story could help even one person avoid the trap I had fallen into, it would be worth it.

I started by joining groups and forums related to gold trading, investment opportunities, and international business. I shared my story with anyone who would listen, and slowly but surely, people began to take notice. My posts were shared, my warnings were heeded, and I began receiving messages from people all over the world. Some were curious, others were skeptical, and many were in the same position I had been in—on the verge of making a life-altering mistake. They reached out to me, asking for advice, wanting to know if the opportunities they were being offered were legitimate. I did my best to help them, to guide them, and to keep them from falling into the same trap that had cost me so much.

One of the most rewarding aspects of this mission was hearing from people who had been saved by my warnings. There were individuals from India, Nepal, Dubai, Bangladesh, and many other countries who had been targeted by scammers, just like I had been. They had seen my posts, read my story, and realized that they were being deceived. They reached out to thank me, to tell me that my story had saved them from losing their money, their time, and their dreams. It was these messages that kept me going, that made me realize that my pain had a purpose.

There was a young man from India who had been about to invest his life savings in a gold deal in Africa. He contacted me after reading one of my posts, asking if the people he was dealing with sounded familiar. As he described the situation, it became clear to me that he was dealing with the same type of scammers who had targeted me. I told him everything I knew, and he decided to back out of the deal. A few weeks later, he messaged me again, thanking me for saving him from what would have been a devastating loss. Stories like his gave me a sense of purpose, a reason to keep sharing my experience, no matter how painful it was to revisit those memories.

Another case that stands out was a woman from Nepal who had been approached by a man claiming to be a gold trader. She had already made an initial payment and was about to travel to Africa to complete the deal when she came across my story. She reached out to me, and I warned her about the dangers she was facing. With my guidance, she managed to cut off contact with the scammers and avoid further loss. She was able to recover some of her money, and she expressed her gratitude to me for helping her see the truth before it was too late.

The more I shared my story, the more I realized just how widespread these scams were. There were countless people being targeted, all over the world, and many of them were completely unaware of the dangers. I began to collaborate with others who had similar experiences, creating a network of individuals dedicated to exposing gold scams and warning potential victims. Together, we were able to reach even more people, to spread our message further, and to make it more difficult for scammers to operate.

Raising awareness became my mission, my purpose. It was a way for me to turn my pain into something positive, to use my experience to help others. It wasn't about seeking revenge against those who had wronged me—it was about making sure that their lies and deceit couldn't continue to harm others. I wanted to shine a light on the dark side of the gold trade, to show people that the promises of quick wealth and easy money were nothing more than traps designed to exploit the trusting and the hopeful.

The journey wasn't without its challenges. There were times when I faced backlash, when people accused me of trying to discredit legitimate businesses or of being bitter about my own failure. But I knew the truth, and I knew that what I was doing was making a difference. For every negative comment, there were dozens of messages of gratitude, of people thanking me for opening their eyes, for saving them from a costly mistake. Those messages were what mattered, and they were what kept me going.

Over time, my efforts began to gain recognition. My story was shared on various platforms, and I was invited to speak on webinars and online forums about gold scams and fraud prevention. I connected with journalists, investigators, and even law enforcement officials who were interested in learning more about the scams I had encountered. I provided them with information, shared my experiences, and worked with them to raise awareness on a larger scale. It felt like, finally, something good was coming out of the nightmare I had endured.

One of the most meaningful moments of this journey was when I received a message from a man in Dubai who had been on the verge of making a significant investment in a gold deal. He had come across my story just in time, and after reading about my experiences, he realized that he was dealing with the same kind of scammers. He thanked me for sharing my story, telling me that I had saved him from making the biggest mistake of his life. It was moments like these that reminded me why I had started this mission in the first place.

Helping others avoid the same fate I had suffered gave me a sense of purpose that I had lost during my time in Uganda. It allowed me to reclaim my life, to find a way to move forward despite everything I had lost. The scars of my experience would always be there, but they no longer defined me. Instead, they became a reminder of the strength I had found, the resilience I had developed, and the mission I had embraced.

As I continued my work, I realized that raising awareness wasn't just about warning people about gold scams—it was about empowering them to ask questions, to be cautious, and to protect themselves in a world full of deceit. It was about giving people the tools they needed to make informed decisions, to recognize the warning signs, and to avoid falling victim to those who would take advantage of their trust.

Looking back, my journey had taken me from the heights of hope to the depths of despair, and finally, to a place of purpose and determination. I had lost everything, but I had also found something invaluable—a mission that gave meaning to my pain and a reason to keep fighting. Awareness had become my mission, and through it, I was able to turn my darkest moments into a beacon of hope for others.

Chapter 15

Starting Over in India

Returning to India was a bittersweet experience. I had finally escaped the nightmare that had consumed my life in Uganda, but I was also faced with the harsh reality of everything I had lost. My home, my business, my financial stability—they were all gone, and I had to start over from scratch. It was a daunting task, but it was also an opportunity to rebuild, to learn from the mistakes I had made, and to create a new life for myself.

The first few weeks back in India were incredibly challenging. I had nowhere to live, no source of income, and a mountain of debt that weighed heavily on my shoulders. My first priority was finding a place to stay. I reached out to friends and family, and eventually, I was able to find temporary accommodation with a relative who was kind enough to take me in. It wasn't ideal, but it gave me the stability I needed to start planning my next steps.

Once I had a roof over my head, I turned my attention to finding work. My old garment and footwear business had been successful once, and I believed that I could rebuild it. But it wasn't going to be easy. My reputation had taken a hit, and many of my old contacts were hesitant to work with me again. I had to prove myself all over again, to show that I was trustworthy and capable. I started small, reaching out to former clients, explaining my situation, and offering my services at a discounted rate. Slowly but surely, I began to regain their trust.

Rebuilding the business was a slow and often frustrating process. There were days when it felt like I was making no progress at all, when the setbacks seemed overwhelming. But I refused to give up. I had faced far greater challenges during my time in Uganda, and I knew that if I could survive that, I could survive this. I threw myself into my work, determined to rebuild not just my business, but my life. I knew that it would take time, but I was willing to put in the effort.

One of the most important lessons I had learned from my experience in Uganda was the value of resilience. There had been so many moments when I had felt like giving up, when the obstacles seemed insurmountable. But I had found a way to keep going, to push through the fear and the pain, and to keep moving forward. That same resilience was what drove me now. I knew that starting over wouldn't be easy, but I also knew that I had the strength to do it.

As the months went by, I began to see progress. I was able to secure a small workspace, and I started to receive more orders from clients. My business was slowly coming back to life, and with each small success, my confidence grew. It wasn't the same as it had been before—I was operating on a much smaller scale, and I was far more cautious in my dealings—but it was a start. And for the first time in a long time, I felt hopeful about the future.

The experience in Uganda had changed me in many ways. I was no longer the naive person who believed in easy money and quick success. I had seen firsthand the darkness that could exist in the world, the people who would stop at nothing to exploit others for their own gain. But I had also seen the kindness of strangers, the people who had helped me when I had nothing. Those experiences had shaped me, had made me more cautious, but also more compassionate. I knew what it was like to be at rock bottom, and I was determined to help others who found themselves in similar situations.

In addition to rebuilding my business, I continued my mission of raising awareness about gold scams. I knew that there were still countless people out there who were at risk of falling into the same trap I had. I used my social media platforms to share my story, to warn others, and to provide guidance to those who needed it. It became a part of who I was, a way to make sure that everything I had been through hadn't been in vain. Helping others gave me a sense of purpose, a reason to keep moving forward, even when things were tough.

The road to recovery was long, and there were many setbacks along the way. There were times when I doubted myself, when I wondered if I would ever be able to fully rebuild what I had lost. But each time I faced a setback, I reminded myself of everything I had already overcome. I had survived threats, betrayal, and loss on a scale I had never imagined possible. I had faced the darkest moments of my life and come out the other side. That knowledge gave me the strength to keep going, to keep fighting for the life I wanted to build.

Looking back, starting over in India was one of the hardest things I had ever done. But it was also one of the most rewarding. It taught me the true meaning of resilience, of perseverance, and of hope. It showed me that no matter how much I had lost, I still had the ability to rebuild, to create something new out of the ashes of my past. And while I would never forget the pain and the loss, I also knew that those experiences had made me stronger, had given me the tools I needed to face whatever challenges lay ahead.

Today, my business is slowly growing, and I am beginning to regain the stability I once had. It's not the same as it was before, but it's a start. And more importantly, I am using my experiences to help others, to warn them, to guide them, and to make sure that they don't have to go through what I went through. Starting over was never going to be easy, but it was the only choice I had. And step by step, I am building a new life—one that is defined not by what I have lost, but by what I have overcome.

Conclusion: A Lesson in Resilience

Reflecting on my journey, I am struck by the profound lessons that emerged from the most harrowing experiences of my life. What began as a hopeful venture into the gold trade turned into a nightmare of deceit, betrayal, and loss. I was scammed, threatened, robbed, and left isolated in a foreign country with seemingly no way out. But from the ashes of that experience, I found a way to rebuild my life, to learn, and to grow stronger.

The first lesson I learned was the importance of due diligence. In the excitement of a new opportunity, I overlooked the warning signs, trusted the wrong people, and failed to verify the authenticity of the business I was getting involved in. If I had taken the time to thoroughly investigate, to ask the right questions, and to seek out independent verification, I might have avoided the devastating losses I experienced. I now know that trust must be earned, and that in any business venture, especially one involving international trade, caution is paramount.

I also learned the value of resilience. There were countless times when I felt like giving up, when the obstacles before me seemed insurmountable. I had lost everything—my money, my business, my home—and yet, I found a way to keep going. It wasn't easy, and there were moments when I doubted myself, when the weight of the loss felt too heavy to bear. But each time I was knocked down, I got back up. I refused to let the actions of others define me or determine my future. That resilience became my greatest strength, and it is what allowed me to start over, to rebuild, and to move forward.

Another important lesson I took away from this experience was the power of community and the kindness of strangers. When I was at my lowest point, it was the unexpected kindness of people like Samuel, the hotel manager, and his girlfriend, that gave me the strength to keep going. They offered me shelter, support, and hope when I had nothing left. It reminded me that even in the darkest of times, there are good people in the world—people who are willing to help others without expecting anything in return. Their kindness inspired me to do the same, to use my experience to help others who might find themselves in similar situations.

My journey has also taught me the importance of sharing my story. For a long time, I felt ashamed of what had happened, embarrassed that I had been deceived so thoroughly. But I came to realize that my story could serve as a warning to others, that by sharing my experience, I could help prevent others from falling into the same trap. It became my mission to raise awareness about gold scams, to educate people about the tactics scammers use, and to empower them to protect themselves. Turning my pain into a mission gave me a sense of purpose, a reason to keep fighting even when things seemed hopeless.

To anyone considering an international business venture, my advice is simple: be cautious, do your research, and never let the promise of quick wealth cloud your judgment. Scammers prey on those who are eager and trusting, and they are skilled at creating convincing illusions. Always seek independent verification, consult experts, and be wary of deals that seem too good to be true. The risks are real, and the consequences can be devastating.

But above all, I want to emphasize the importance of resilience. Life is unpredictable, and setbacks are inevitable. There will be times when you are faced with challenges that seem impossible to overcome, times when you feel like giving up. But it is in those moments that true strength is found. The ability to keep going, to get back up after being knocked down, is what defines us. My journey has been filled with pain and loss, but it has also been a journey of growth, of finding strength I didn't know I had, and of discovering a new purpose.

Starting over was never easy, but it was the only choice I had. And through that process, I learned that we are capable of far more than we realize. We can endure, we can adapt, and we can rebuild. My story is not just a story of loss—it is a story of resilience, of hope, and of the power of the human spirit to overcome even the greatest of challenges. And as I continue to rebuild my life, I am determined to use my experience to help others, to raise awareness, and to be a beacon of hope for those who may be facing their own struggles.

In the end, the greatest lesson I learned is that no matter how much you lose, as long as you are still standing, you have the power to rebuild. The scars of my past will always be there, but they are a testament to my resilience, to my ability to overcome. And for that, I am grateful.

Author's Note: A Message of Gratitude to My Readers

As I bring this journey to a close, I find myself filled with a deep sense of gratitude for each and every one of you who has taken the time to read my story. Your willingness to share in my experiences, to reflect on my challenges, and to understand the lessons I've learned means more to me than words can express.

This journey has been filled with unexpected turns—both moments of despair and glimpses of hope. At times, it felt like I had lost everything. But through it all, I discovered resilience, kindness, and the ability to start over. Sharing my story was not easy, but knowing that it might serve as a warning or inspiration for someone else made it all worthwhile. It is my hope that my experiences can help you see that even in the darkest times, there is a way forward.

To those who have supported me, whether through kind words, encouragement, or simply by reading my story, I want to say thank you. Your support has been a beacon of light in my darkest moments, and I am eternally grateful. To those who may be struggling, facing your own challenges, I want to remind you that you are not alone. There is strength within you that you may not yet realize, and there are people in this world who care and who are willing to help.

This book is not just my story—it is a testament to the power of resilience, the importance of due diligence, and the incredible kindness of strangers. It is a reminder that no matter how much you lose, as long as you have the courage to keep moving forward, you can rebuild. Thank you for allowing me to share my journey with you, and for being a part of my healing and growth.

I wish you all strength, hope, and the courage to face whatever challenges come your way. Remember, no matter what happens, you have the power to rise again.

With deepest appreciation,

Arun Kumar Verma